THE RIVER Avon

A JOURNEY FOLLOWING THE RIVER FROM
TEWKESBURY TO ITS SOURCE

Hunt End Books
66 Enfield Road, Hunt End, Redditch
Worcestershire B97 5NH
First published in Great Britain by
Hunt End Books 2006

ISBN 0-9549813-1-6

Acknowledgements
The publisher would like to thank those who helped
with the prepration of this book or gave
permission to reproduce illustrations and photographs:
Anne Bradford
Barry Crowther
Evesham Library
The Lower Avon Navigation Trust Limited
Patsy Lane
The Shakespeare Birthplace Trust Record Office

Printed in England by
Goodman Baylis Limited
London Road
Worcester WR5 2JH

Front cover: Saxon Mill and the river Avon. A 17th century timber-framed and stone mill house, combined with a house of 1822, is now a popular inn and restaurant.

Frontispiece: The river Avon, covered with the flowers and pads of our native yellow water lily, near Cleeve Hill.

Back cover: The Royal Shakespeare Theatre at Stratford-upon-Avon was designed by Elizabeth Scott and completed in 1932. An earlier theatre, opened on Shakespeare's birthday in 1879, was destroyed by fire in 1926.

CONTENTS

THE RIVER Avon

A JOURNEY FOLLOWING THE RIVER FROM TEWKESBURY TO ITS SOURCE

Text, photography and design by
John Bradford

Hunt End Books

The dotted line on this map represents the route followed along the river Avon from Tewkesbury to Naseby.

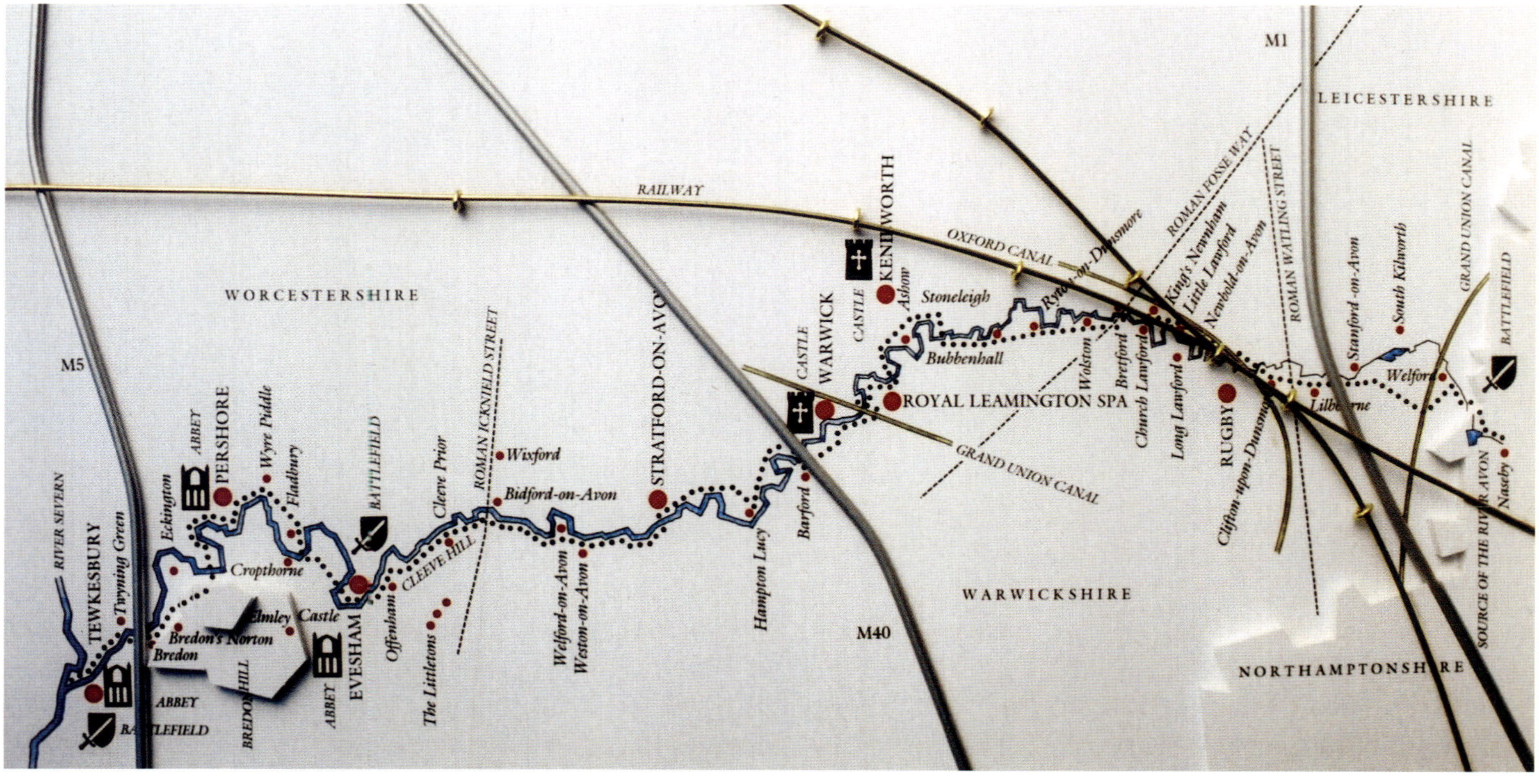

Introduction

It is a misty morning in the centre of Britain sometime after the Roman legions have been recalled to defend Rome. A little group of people stand beside a river talking in the Celtic language. Out of the mist there emerges on the opposite bank a party of migrant Saxons. Warily, the two groups attempt to converse but neither speaks the other's language. Pointing at the river, the Saxons convey to the Celts that they want to know what it is called. 'Afon' say the Celts, thinking to themselves, ' What sort of halfwits are these who don't recognise a river (or 'afon') when they see one?'. The Saxons eventually become the dominant culture in these parts and the river for ever more is known as the Avon, or in effect, the river River! This, of course, is speculation but is, I suggest, as plausible an account of the confusion arising from the naming of the river as any other. In Wales, of course, where the Celtic people continued to be the dominant race, Afon is still the prefix to the name of all rivers as is evident on any OS maps of that country.

The Avon flows through England's history. For 900 years from the 7th century, the monastic movement was a significant influence on the early life of the nation. The great abbeys of Tewkesbury, Pershore and Evesham, all founded between 681 and 715, were centres of discipline, faith and piety (as well as, from time to time, indiscipline, worldliness and impiety). They also preserved and developed practical skills such as architecture, hydraulic engineering, sanitation, agriculture, husbandry, ironworking and milling.

Three significant and bloody battles took place beside the river Avon. Two of these, the barons' rebellion in 1265 at Evesham, and the Civil War battle of Naseby in 1645 were conflicts about the claims of absolute power by kings. The other, at Tewkesbury, in 1471, was a dynastic struggle between the red rose of Lancaster and the white rose of York.

Two of England's mightiest castles, Warwick on the banks of the Avon and nearby Kenilworth, played major roles in the life of the nation. At Warwick, the illustrious Beauchamp dynasty provided soldiers and statesmen for a succession of kings, whilst building for themselves one of the most formidable fortresses in the land. Kenilworth Castle was owned by a succession of kings, notably John, Henry IV and Henry V, but the period for which it is best remembered is the reign of Elizabeth I who was entertained there by her favourite, Robert Dudley, in 1575. For nineteen days she was treated to a series of glittering pageants and spectacles performed on the large artificial lake surrounding the castle, interspersed with days of hunting in the forest.

Stratford-upon-Avon's most famous son, William Shakespeare, is buried in the Collegiate Church of the Holy Trinity beside the Avon. His name is revered around the world, often by those who care little for England's history but come in their thousands every year to see his plays performed at the Royal Shakespeare Theatre and to visit the various buildings associated with his family.

Together with Royal Leamington Spa, a town of elegant 19th century squares and terraces, and Rugby with its famous public school, these are the attractions that feature prominently in the tourist guides to the Avon valley, but there is much more to be seen near to the Avon; Bredon Hill and its pretty villages, a little piece of the Cotswolds that got left behind in Worcestershire when the Cotswolds slipped away eastwards; the great medieval tithe barns at Bredon and Middle Littleton; many fine village churches, some on the banks of the Avon, like Ashow, Bubbenhall and Newbold; churches with exceptional treasures like Cropthorne with its ninth century Saxon crosshead. There are the great houses of Charlecote Park, Stoneleigh Abbey and Stanford Hall, and at Guy's Cliff, below the eerie ruins of a Georgian mansion, a riverside cave is the location for the once famous twelfth century romantic legend of Guy of Warwick.

But if I had to identify places by the Avon that left a lasting impression on me, they might well include some that were well away from the tourist trail, like St Catherine's chapel and well at the foot of Bredon Hill's escarpment, once the haunt of wolves, though all trace of both wolves and chapel are long gone. Another would be the tiny depopulated village of Kings Newnham with its ruined church, monks' fishponds and remains of a watermill beside the river. These and many other hidden places amply reward those who are willing to explore the area on foot.

This journey was made between late winter and the following autumn and it was my intention that the changing seasons should be reflected in the book's sequence of photographs. However, it is by no means unusual for our English winter to wait until spring flowers are in full bloom before throwing its worst at us, as was the case in the year of my journey. Sharp-eyed readers may notice one or two other photographs that are out of season, either for reasons beyond my control or because the pictures chose themselves.

John Bradford

The confluence of the rivers Avon, left, and Severn at Tewkesbury.

Rose hips, a rich source of vitamin C, were picked during the Second World War by school children who were paid 3d a pound by the Ministry of Health.

Nafford mill was gutted by a terrible fire on 17th May 1909 which left only the four outer walls standing.
Image courtesy of Evesham Library, 'The Ward Collection'.

THE RIVER Avon
TEWKESBURY TO EVESHAM

Abbeys and apple blossom

Tewkesbury

At Tewkesbury the domesticated Avon flows into the feral Severn. The Avon's natural confluence with the Severn can be found a little to the north-west of the town, but a branch of the river, called the Mill Avon, thought to have been cut by monks in the twelfth century to power the abbey's mill, flows behind the town and joins the Severn about a mile further south. Although no longer a working mill, Abbey Mill is still there, having been rebuilt in 1793. It is now a restaurant.

A small Benedictine monastery founded in 715 at Tewkesbury was twice burnt down by Danish invaders. The present abbey was consecrated in 1121 and was built largely of stone brought down the Avon on barges from quarries on Bredon Hill.

This journey begins at the abbey, a building that, in my view, is unsurpassed along the entire length of the river. Perhaps, however, I should declare an interest. I am an enthusiastic admirer of Romanesque church architecture, preferring the round arch to the pointed, or Gothic arch. Tewkesbury Abbey is an outstanding example of Romanesque style. Within the Abbey a colonnade of monumental columns thirty feet high and six feet in diameter fills the nave, each one supporting an arch, that in turn supports a triforium with twin arches to each bay. The effect is as intended - awe-inspiring. Outside, the 148 feet high tower, the largest and finest Romanesque tower in the country, is decorated near the top with a graceful interlaced blind arcade. The overall impression, both outside and in, is of power and majesty tempered by restraint (although 'restraint', a modern virtue, was no doubt unintended by the builders).

By the time of the dissolution of the monasteries in 1540, Tewkesbury Abbey had become one of the richest religious houses in the country. Henry VIII was persuaded by the town's inhabitants to sell the abbey church to them for £453, a considerable sum of money in those days, this being the estimated value of the lead on the roof and the bells. So it is thanks to the generosity of the people of Tewkesbury that the Abbey did not suffer the fate of so many other religious houses.

Tewkesbury's trade benefited from its position beside the meeting of two rivers. By the 16th century it had four mills, but the previously flourishing cloth trade was in decline. The town turned to stocking-making in many of the back-alley hovels behind the main streets, and it is estimated that by the early 19th century, one in four people were employed in the trade. Today the hovels have gone but the alleys remain and are a distinctive feature of the town. A further characteristic of Tewkesbury is the many three and four-storey houses along the main streets. These high-rise houses were the answer to the town's confined position between four rivers which then, as now, often flooded. The town has a number of historic inns, the oldest, the Old Black Bear dating from 1308.

A fascinating painting of Tewkesbury's quay, dated 21st April 1804, hangs in the offices of the Town Council. It depicts the busy quayside with several moored trows, from one of which large barrels are being rolled down planks on to the quay. In the foreground teams of horses harnessed to carts full of coal are about to depart. Elsewhere, fishermen's nets hang out to dry and in the far distance can be seen the square sails of two trows on the river Avon.

Tewkesbury Abbey viewed from the flooded river Swilgate.

Tewkesbury is famous for the decisive battle of the Wars of the Roses on 4th May 1471. Edward IV of the Yorkist faction, whose emblem was a white rose, commanded an army of 5,000. Facing him was the 6,000 strong army of Queen Margaret of Anjou, the wife of Henry VI. Her emblem was the red rose of Lancaster and her ambition was to place her son, Prince Edward, on the throne of England. King Edward's army, although inferior in numbers, was better equipped and armed. He outmanoeuvred his enemy causing them to flee in panic, some towards the river Severn and Bloody Meadow, others to find sanctuary in the Abbey. Margaret's son, Edward, was killed in the battle, so ending all hope for the Lancastrian cause.

Prince Edward's body was buried in the Abbey choir, a somewhat surprisingly magnanimous event for those times when it was more common for the bodies of the defeated to be hacked to pieces and displayed in public as a warning to others who might be plotting against the victors. Those who had sought sanctuary in the Abbey were tried, removed and executed in the town at the High Cross. This was demolished in 1650 and is now the site of the war memorial. Margaret was captured and imprisoned until ransomed by the King of France. Her husband, Henry VI, was less fortunate. He was executed in the Tower of London.

Right: Fourteen columns 30 feet high and 6 feet in diameter support Romanesque arches inside the Abbey. The 14th century vault has fifteen bosses illustrating the life of Christ. Tombs include those of Abbot Alan who wrote an eye-witness account of the martyrdom of Thomas Becket. The de Clares, Dispensers and Beauchamps who all extended and rebuilt the abbey are buried here, as are the Duke of Clarence and his wife.

Far right: The Abbey towering above the rooftops of shops built in the late 15th century as a commercial venture for the Benedictine monastery. On the right is 66 Church Street, built in 1475 and recently restored and painted with a traditional limewash.

Tewkesbury Abbey's Norman tower and 14th century ambulatory.

Left: The Royal Hop Pole, one of the town's coaching inns where Charles Dickens' Mr Pickwick dined.

Right and below left: Timber-framed buildings in the town.

Below right: The High Street.

Lilley's Alley

Tewkesbury originally had 90 alleyways of which 30 remain today. Long and narrow, they acted as drains and rubbish dumps and were often the only source of light for many households. Cholera and diphtheria spread rapidly in the damp and crowded conditions during the 18th and 19th centuries.

Fletcher's Alley

Fish Alley

Yarnell's Alley

Compton's Alley

Wall's Court

Baptists were persecuted for their religious beliefs during the second half of the 17th century when many were imprisoned and sentenced to death. They tried to avoid detection by meeting in small groups in buildings that were disguised as private houses. This is the origin of the Old Baptist Chapel in the court that bears its name, a 15th century three-bay timber-framed hall house, with galleries at either end. A domestic setting for worship by small groups of family and friends suited the Baptists' beliefs very well. They

rejected the formality and ritual of the established church and consequently had to meet secretly, conducting baptisms during services held at night. Tewkesbury's Old Baptist Chapel is probably the first in southern England.

Below: The Old Black Bear claims to be the county's oldest public house.

Right: A distinguished-looking timber-framed house with a ground floor shop in the High Street.

Far right: The House of the Nodding Gables, once the stage coach ticket office. The hanging key dates from the days when it was an ironmonger's shop.

Right: Lock gates provide access from the Mill Avon to the river Avon and the river Severn

Tewkesbury's marina and weir.

Tewkesbury to Bredon Hill

It was late winter and a fierce north-westerly wind was threatening to freeze-dry my lungs as I set off from Tewkesbury to walk along the west bank of the Avon towards Twyning Green. The county boundary between Worcestershire and Gloucestershire follows this stretch of the river as far as Bredon, where it loops westward, then south along the river Severn back to Tewkesbury, so enclosing a peninsular of Gloucestershire within Worcestershire. For the next two miles only, I was in Gloucestershire.

Two cormorants flew up from the river as I approached and a quartet of great-crested grebes made a welcome appearance, all attracted, perhaps, to the area by its proximity to the lakes at Bredons Hardwick. On the opposite bank of the river a few Greylag geese were socialising amiably with the ubiquitous flock of Canada geese. Cleaning my boots that evening, I pondered whether I might have discovered a new wonder adhesive. Mud, grass and goose droppings proved to be a formidable combination, not dissimilar to the ingredients of daub, as in 'medieval wattle and daub'.

Unfortunately there is no longer a ferry between the Fleet Inn at Twyning Green and the lane on the opposite bank of the river, so my chosen route had to await another day.

A pleasant walk along a broad flood bank beside the Avon leads to Bredon. A pair of oyster catchers (not a bird I automatically associate with Worcestershire) darted away from a muddy ledge of the river, uttering their shrill, piping call.

Bredon is notable for both its church and 13th century tithe barn. The Saxon church was destroyed by the Danes in approximately 850 AD and the present building erected between the 12th and 14th centuries. It has a slender spire that is a landmark for miles around. In the south aisle there is an alabaster and black marble monument to Sir Giles and Lady Catherine Reed who died in 1611. The ornate splendour no doubt does justice to the local noble family whose descendants founded the 17th century almshouses in the village. More to my taste, however, was the early 14th century stone coffin lid relocated to its present position against the wall of the sanctuary. It features a cross of thorn with portraits of a man and woman, possibly ancestors of the Reed family. Stylistically, this reminds me of contemporary illustrated manuscripts. It exhibits a similar love of ornament occupying airy space.

The villages encircling Bredon Hill are celebrated for their beauty. Bredon, Overbury, Kemerton, Bredons Norton, Great Comberton, Little Comberton and Elmley Castle are all within easy walking distance of the Avon, whilst Ashton-under-Hill and Beckford on the eastern side of the hill are, I feel, too distant to be included in this journey. Happily, unlike one or two of their Cotswold neighbours, they are as yet unspoilt by commercialisation.

In striking contrast to the surrounding Worcestershire countryside of hedged fields, and brick and timber houses, Bredon Hill's villages are largely built using the local honey-coloured stone, or timber and stone. The hillside fields, similarly, are enclosed with locally-quarried dry-stone walls. Like the hill itself, Bredon's villages look like escapees from the nearby Cotswolds.

The river Avon near Tewkesbury.

Snowdrops are a rather mysterious plant. There is some doubt as to whether they are a true native of Britain, conditions here being too cold in February, when the plant flowers, for insects to act as pollinators. They therefore must rely for reproduction on offshoot bulbs from the old one. Unlike most other wild flowers, snowdrops are usually found in isolated colonies in the vicinity of churches, ruined abbeys, priories and nunneries. This suggests that the flower may have had a religious significance and was brought here from continental Europe. Cottage gardens also provide a frequent refuge, indeed their presence is often an indication that a long-vanished building once occupied the site. On damp grey days in late January there is no more cheering sight than the sea-green spears of snowdrops forcing their way through cold earth, soon to be capped by a myriad nodding, green-fringed, pure white flowers. They are the heralds of seasonal change reminding us that spring's multi-coloured battalions are on their way.

Right: A milestone dated 1808 near the entrance to the village.

Above: In 1875, a dray drawn by two horses, together with the drayman and the ferryman, were crossing the river at this point on a rather suspect ferry. Nearing the other side, the horses panicked, plunging into the river and taking the dray and drayman with them. The ferryman managed to save the drayman but both horses were drowned.

Right: Bredon's 13th century tithe barn, 124 feet long, with aisles and two porches, one with an upper room and fireplace, is unique in the county of Worcestershire.

Right: The alabaster memorial to Sir Giles Reed and his wife, Catherine, dominates the south chapel of Bredon's church.

Right: Avon Cottage, Bredon.

Below: Bredon's church is dedicated to St Giles, one of the most popular saints of the Middle Ages, patron of cripples, lepers and beggars.

Above: An early 14th century coffin lid, possibly featuring portraits of early members of the Reed family.

Left: A cottage at Bredons Norton.

Below: Cottages at the entrance to Manor Lane, Little Comberton.

Right: St Peter's Church, Little Comberton, is said to be built on the site of a Roman temple, artefacts from that time having been found in the churchyard. Its north doorway has a curious tympanum featuring a cross and eight whorls.

Below: A narrow bench inside the porch has outlines of hands and a shield engraved into the stone, which are thought to be the hands of newly-married 18th century brides. The shield bears the date 1733 and the letters WD.

Left: Elmley Castle, from which the village takes its name, belonged to the Beauchamp family. When they moved to Warwick the castle fell into decay and by the mid-16th century John Leland, passing that way, noted that he 'saw carts caringe stone thens to amend Pershore Bridge'. By the time of Elizabeth I's visit, the castle had disappeared.

Below: Stone carvings of a rabbit and pig inside the porch of St Mary's Church date from the 11th or 12th century.

Left: In 1575 Queen Elizabeth visited the Savage family whose support for her grandfather, Henry Tudor, had been rewarded with a grant of propert at Elmley Castle. This exquisitely-carved alabaster monument in the village church is of Sir William Savage, his son, Sir Giles, and Sir William's wife, Lady Catherine, who is holding an infant daughter born after his death. Their four sons kneel at the foot of the memorial. The church font is supported by fearsome-looking dragons carved in the 11th or 12th century.

The site of St Catherine's Chapel is situated at the foot of the escarpment, just below the summit of Bredon Hill. Very little, if anything, remains to be seen now, but when it was excavated in 1920 medieval foundations were found overlying earlier, probably Saxon, foundations. Documentary evidence from 779 and 972 refer to a village called Woollashill at the top of the hill. The name is derived from the packs of wolves that roamed the wild uplands of Bredon Hill. St Catherine's Spring and well can still be seen nearby - the spring, unhappily, redirected via pipes into animal drinking troughs. The chapel is reputed to have been founded by Sir Richard de Muchgros, who also founded the manor of Woollas Hall in the early 13th century. Woollas Hall (above) is well below the chapel, and the house we see today was the creation of John Hanford in 1611.

A hillside spring near St Catherine's Chapel.

Bredon Hill to Nafford

When Bredon Hill puts on his hat
Men of the Vale, beware of that.
If it rain on Good Friday, and Easter Day,
There'll be plenty of grass, but little good hay.
If Candlemas Day be cloudy and black,
It carries the winter away on its back.

Bredon Hill is one of a number of outliers left behind by the receding Cotswold escarpment. Like a great layer cake of Jurassic limestone and sands and clays, the Cotswolds tilt north-west to south-east. Consequently, the softer, less stable sands and clays gradually slide backwards, leaving behind the escarpment and a number of isolated hills.

Bredon's hilltop Iron Age fort is well over 2,000 years old, some of its occupants coming to a violent end, judging by the fifty skeletons found there during archaeological excavations. Finds of coins suggest the fortifications were later taken over by the Romans. The earthworks are still very impressive. Less so is Parsons Folly, a tower erected on the hill's summit by a Mr Parsons of Kemerton, who wanted to increase, by artificial means, the height of the hill to 1,000 feet. It is visible from many distant parts of Worcestershire.

Many footpaths criss-cross the hill, all starting at the villages and hamlets round its base. From Great Comberton a steep path ending in an enjoyable little scramble to the Iron Age earthworks, is one of my preferred routes. From Netherton Fields, near Elmley Castle, the Wychavon Way climbs through fields and woods to the top of the hill, passing the site of the demolished castle on the way. It then follows the edge of an east-facing escarpment before descending to Ashton-under-Hill. The tracks with the easiest gradients are found on the southern slops of Bredon Hill, but all have one thing in common, they converge at the tower and the Banbury Stone.

I have walked Bredon Hill repeatedly during the last twenty years or so. It is a particular favourite of mine, as well as being conveniently situated not far from my home. This was the hill on which I introduced my daughter, then six years old, to the pleasures of hill-walking. Stuffing an apple into my pocket in case she wanted a snack, we set off up the hill. With two teenage sons, I had some experience of the prodigious amounts of food boys could put away, but I was clearly insufficiently informed about the appetites of small girls. The apple was hungrily devoured, core, pips and all.

Snow, in the year of this walk, fell in Scotland, the north of England, northern Ireland and East Anglia. It fell as far south as Staffordshire and the inland counties of Shropshire and Herefordshire, but the Avon valley remained snowless. A television weather presenter, ankle-deep in snow, stood in front of a waist-high drift, struggling with her hair which was being blown across her eyes by a horizontal wind. She assured us that all parts of the country would soon have snow. Still the Avon valley remained snowless. As a photographer I found this disappointing. One of the aims of this book was seasonal variety in the pictures, and I was counting on snow to work its usual winter magic. At last, in late February, snow arrived in the Midlands, blown in from Scandinavia, together with daytime temperatures hovering around zero. It was not, however, Christmas card type snow - long blue shadows on sparkling white, beneath an impossibly blue sky. This was blizzard-type snow falling from low grey clouds scudding along the summit of Bredon Hill. As I laboured upwards, desperately trying to protect my camera from the driving snow, Bredon's escarpment made fleeting appearances when the clouds thinned, only to be hidden again moments later. A fox, almost black against the white landscape, fled from me downhill, its long tail streaming out behind. Moments later a herd of fallow deer, also startled by my sudden appearance, sprinted soundlessly to the shelter of a patch of black leafless hawthorns and sloes.

From Bredons Norton a narrow road dwindling to a rough track with cattle grids winds round the western flank of Bredon Hill to Woollas Hall, then descends to join the road to Nafford and the river Avon.

Left: Freezing fog on the Avon near Eckington.

Facing page: Snow on Bredon Hill, its summit hidden by drifting low cloud.

Above: A wintry sun bursts briefly through dense freezing fog on Bredon Hill.

Left: Frost-encrusted coarse grass on the slopes of Bredon Hill.

Facing page: Trees on Bredon Hill, near the site of Elmley Castle, from which the nearby village takes its name.

Below: The summit of Bredon Hill provides stunning views of the river Avon, Great Comberton and Pershore, as well as the Malvern Hills to the west. There was a landing stage, reached via Quay Lane in Great Comberton, where corn was loaded onto boats to be taken down-river to Nafford Mill. The site of the landing stage may still be seen but the mill was destroyed by fire on 17th May 1909.

Right: As late as the 18th century the King and Queen stones on Bredon Hill were still being ceremonially whitewashed for meetings of the Court Leet of the Oswoldslow Hundred that assembled there to dispense local justice.

Facing page: Parson's Folly on the summit of Bredon Hill, viewed from Eckington.

Right: The waters of the Avon pouring through sluice gates at Nafford.

Nafford to Pershore

The Gwen Finch Wetland Nature Reserve at Nafford was created between 1999 and 2001. It consists of four large scrapes, three of which are planted with reeds. Water for the site is pumped from the Berwick Brook by two wind pumps. Otters now frequent the reserve and many birds breed there, including redshank, yellow wagtail and reed warbler. There is no public access.

Visitors enter the churchyard of St James at Birlingham through a stone arch, originally the chancel arch in a Norman church that was demolished in 1871 to make way for the present building. This, and the perpendicular tower, are all that are left of the old church. In February the stone wall enclosing St James' churchyard barely succeeds in containing a riot of flowering snowdrops overflowing on to the roadside verge.

Tenth century 'Eccyncgtune', twelfth century 'Aichintune', fourteenth century 'Ekyngton' or modern Eckington is a village with one of the oldest bridges in Worcestershire. Various authors give wildly differing dates for its age, but I shall settle for Niklaus Pevsner who says it is fifteenth or sixteenth century. Built of red sandstone, it has refuges above cut-water piers and replaced a bridge erected in 1440.

Holy Trinity Church was built in the thirteenth century but the preaching cross in the village is of even greater antiquity. In 1774 a gallery was installed at the west end of the church's nave, and this was enlarged in 1841 to provide space for singers, two violins, two cellos, one bass viol, flutes, 'clarionets', trumpet, trombone and bassoon. Ecclesiastical fashions in music come and go and by 1887 the gallery had been demolished, as had the musicians. The choir and congregation were now to be accompanied by a new organ. As a boy I sang in the choir of an ancient village church in Shropshire and on a recent visit, I was not surprised to learn that the choir had been disbanded many years ago. Several local churches now have to share one vicar.

However, some traditions from the distant past are reassuringly familiar. In 1659 a hefty fine of £400 was inflicted on William George of Eckington at Worcester County Sessions for growing and curing tobacco on 400 poles of land (a pole is 5.5 yards or 30.25 square yards). Others also were fined for the same offence.

Left: The Gwen Finch Wetland Nature Reserve at Nafford, with the river Avon in the foreground.

Right: Sunset over the Malvern Hills and the river Avon at Nafford.

Right: Eckington Bridge.

Left: Tiddesley Wood, near Pershore, is celebrated for its bluebells. The humidity of Britain's climate, unlike that of Europe, is very much to the flower's liking. Consequently, our woodlands in Spring are filled with the violet-blue of this much-loved flower, a sight almost unique to these islands. The famous Pershore Yellow Egg Plum was first discovered growing wild in Tiddesley Wood in 1827. By the 1870s, following its cultivation, approximately 900 tons, picked by children and their mothers, were being sent to market at harvest time.

Below: More than any other plant, the yellow water lily defines the character of the river Avon. Unlike the river Severn, where it is absent, this native lily may be seen in most parts of the Avon. Its old name 'Brandy Bottle' refers to the shape of the fruit capsule and its alcoholic smell. Here it is seen growing near Pershore.

Pershore

Pershore Abbey is a magnificent fragment of a once magnificent abbey. At the time of the dissolution of the monasteries, the nave of the abbey church was granted to the townspeople as a place of worship, but having first accepted the offer, they later changed their minds and exchanged it for the choir, tower and transepts at a cost of £400. The north transept, unfortunately, fell down in the mid 1600s with the result that the ground plan of the abbey today is quite odd. The impression on entering is of a church that is taller than it is either long or wide. That quibble aside, the building contains many striking features.

The earliest record of a monastery at Pershore dates back to 681 when Ethelred, King of Mercia, provided an endowment. The abbey prospered, in spite of Viking raids, until the end of the tenth century, when two-thirds of its lands were seized by a Mercian earl. They were never returned, and in 1065 Edward the Confessor gave the lands as an endowment to his recently constructed abbey at Westminster. So it was that Pershore became divided between two abbeys and, later, two parishes, each with its own church, one at the abbey and, facing it, Saint Andrews.

Right: Forty-one bosses enliven the quire vault, no two quite the same. Two have faces with foliage growing from their mouths, the so-called 'Green Man' image, widely used from the 13th to 15th centuries and found in many churches throughout the country. Others feature oak, ivy and clusters of grapes inhabited by various small animals.

Left: The Abbey Church faces its old rival, St Andrew's, now a visitors' centre but formerly belonging to the Abbot of Westminster.

Left: Gilbert Scott's bell-ringers' floating platform in Pershore Abbey's lantern tower, described by him as the finest in the country after Lincoln Cathedral.

Below: The war memorial in the Abbey's south transept, a bronze figure of Immortality by Alfred Drury.

The Almonry, where monks gave charity to the poor and housed their visitors. Restored by the Worcestershire Historic Buildings Preservation Trust.

Perhaps the most beautiful feature of the abbey's interior is its quire vault. A good example of 'ploughshare' stone-ribbed groins with intermediate lierne ribs, the intersections are punctuated with wonderfully intricate carved bosses. When the whole abbey was still standing, the view down the 180 feet long Romanesque, ten-bay nave to the quire must have been breathtaking. Following the partial destruction of the abbey church the various 'holes' left were patched up and following the collapse of the north transept in 1686 the tower was reinforced with two huge buttresses. There followed a period of gradual neglect, but by the mid-nineteenth century it was realised that this could not be allowed to continue. Gilbert Scott, the renowned architect, was consulted and reconstruction work began. His most radical change was the removal of the floor of the lantern tower, revealing the decorated tracery panelling, and his design of the 'floating' bell-chamber was truly inspired.

The town is noted for its many Georgian and Regency houses, mostly of red brick, some with canopied balconies.

One of the delights of exploring the English countryside is that of stumbling on the unexpected. Arcade Bookshop, 21 High Street, conceals such a surprise. A flight of steps at the rear of the ground floor descends to a medieval vaulted chapel with a pointed - cinquefoiled 13th century piscina. The room is presently in use as a children's book and toy shop.

Pershore's fourteenth century by-laws make entertaining reading. Inhabitants were forbidden to play tennis, football and 'the dyse'. Those found breaking the law were fined twelve pence. Bakers could only buy grain at the Tuesday market. Dogs had to be kept indoors at night and all tenants were to be home by nine o'clock. Tenants must not allow their workmen or apprentices to play games or frequent taverns on feast days, nor must they restrain their servants or minstrels from attending church services. Everyone's swine and kine must be placed under the charge of the common herd and streets must be thoroughly cleansed once a month.

The old monastic bridge over the Avon at Pershore has happily been preserved with traffic now using the new bridge alongside. At the time of the Civil War, in 1644, King Charles ordered the bridge to be broken down to prevent the parliamentary army from pursuing him. The work was done so hurriedly that some of his army failed to get safely across. A major, three officers and twenty-six men were drowned, as well as eighty countrymen, whose hats floated off down the river.

By 1840, the height of the turnpike era, there were 20,000 miles of roads with milestones. This one in Pershore dates from 1800.

Facing page: A bustling farmers' market in Broad Street. Exceptionally wide with a two-way traffic system either side of car parking spaces, this was until 1836 occupied by houses and a shambles.

Left: Home of the Wilsons, a family of tanners until 1835. The tannery works were behind the house.

Below: 13th century piscina in a vaulted chapel below the Arcade Bookshop in High Street.

Left: Pershore has many elegant Georgian and Regency houses. This one in Bridge Street has a particularly fine hood with decorative swags and foliate brackets.

Left: A house in Bridge Street.

Right: Bedford House, Bridge Street.

Below: Modest but elegant architecture in Broad Street.

Above: Perrott House, built by Judge Perrott in 1770. His repairs to weirs and locks on the Avon brought prosperity to the town at the end of the century.

Left: This private house was once the 'Black Horse Inn', known to have been here before 1743.

Above and facing page: The old medieval bridge, preserved but disused. Darker-coloured stone above the central arch indicates repairs made following the bridge's destruction by King Charles' army in 1644 during the Civil War.

The weir on the Avon at Pershore. Many of the houses in Bridge Street have long narrow gardens ending at the river's edge.

Pershore to Fladbury

Once free of Pershore's modern housing estates, quiet field paths and lanes lead to Fladbury, passing through Wyre Piddle on the way, a village now by-passed by a new section of the main road between Evesham and Worcester. Wyre Piddle has a number of attractive half-timbered houses and a church occupying a prehistoric burial ground. A popular pub, the Anchor Inn, has a terraced garden that descends to the Avon.

Vines were grown at Fladbury, perhaps by the monk to whom 'Fledanburg' was given by Ethelred, King of Mercia, in AD691. The Victoria County History of Worcestershire notes that at the end of the eighteenth century, two acres of land called 'The Vineyard' belonged to the rector of Fladbury. There are two mills in the village, Cropthorne Mill and Fladbury Mill, one each side of the river. Neither is now a working mill. A record of 1086 in the Domesday Book states that a mill at Fladbury was worth ten shillings and twenty stitches of eels a year (twenty eels to the stitch). A later scribe notes in 1302 that the village had two mills worth £3.19s 6d.

Plans to make the Avon navigable were proposed in 1636 by Sir William Sandys who lived in Fladbury. Within three years, at a personal cost of £20,000, work was sufficiently advanced to enable vessels of up to thirty tons to sail between Tewkesbury and Stratford-upon-Avon. Improvements continued and by the mid-eighteenth century the size of vessels had increased to forty tons. Contemporary illustrations show trows and frigates with single masts and square sails being steered by an oar. Restrictions on size were necessitated by the low medieval bridges at Tewkesbury and Eckington, which then, as now, had a maximum headroom of only eight feet. About 400 of these vessels each year used the waterway, carrying coal from the Shropshire pits to destinations along the Avon, and agricultural produce down-river to Gloucester and Bristol. The original sluices and locks were all rebuilt during the twentieth century and today the trows have been replaced by pleasure craft.

A bridge over the Avon connects Fladbury to its near neighbour, Cropthorne. Its name, 'Jubilee Bridge' refers to an earlier bridge built to celebrate the 1887 Jubilee of Queen Victoria. Prior to that, travellers between the two villages had to ford the river.

Right: Primroses and violets flower in early spring. Unlike its cousin, the sweet violet, with one of the most distinctive scents of all wild flowers, the dog violet is without scent.

Above and right: Cottages in Church Street, Wyre Piddle.

Right: A ferry operated at the Anchor Inn until the beginning of the Second World War. Villagers from Wick on the opposite side of the river came across to visit the market at Wyre Piddle that was held under a great elm tree known as the Arbour Oak. The Anchor Inn today is one of the most popular pubs on the banks of the Avon.

Above: This exquisitely delicate fragment of early 12th century stained glass, depicting the Virgin Mary and the infant Christ, is preserved in Fladbury's parish church.

Right: Cropthorne Mill was built at the start of the 18th century, whilst its neighbour on the opposite bank, Fladbury Mill, may date from the 16th century.

Below: The lost art of monumental carving in Fladbury's churchyard.

Right: A fine house in Fladbury, viewed from the churchyard.

Below: Old Fladbury Stores.

Above: Fladbury's ducks enjoying a siesta.

Fladbury to Evesham

Worcestershire is a county noted for its attractive villages, and few can be more pleasing than Cropthorne. It is also a village of great antiquity. The Mercian King Offa, builder of the monumental dyke that separates Wales from England, gave Cropthorne to the Priory of Worcester in 786. The earliest part of St Michael's church, the tower and the chancel arch, date from the twelfth century, but there was almost certainly a church of some kind there before that. The widely admired Cropthorne Cross, described by Niklaus Pevsner as 'the best piece of Anglo-Saxon art in the county', dates from 800 and was discovered embedded in the south wall of the sanctuary in the 18th century.

Cropthorne Court, built on the site of King Offa's summer house, was in the 17th and early 18th centuries, the home of the Dingley family. Old registers, however, record their presence in the form of births, marriages and deaths as far back as the 14th century. Two prominent and flamboyantly decorated tombs inside the church, display painted effigies of Francis and Elizabeth Dingley with their nineteen children, and Edward and Joyce Dingley with their four sons and three daughters. Francis was Sheriff of Worcester and was killed in a duel in 1624. Edward, grandson of Francis, died in 1646. The families' fortunes ended in ignominy and scandal. Eleanor, grand-daughter of Edward and Joyce, married Sir Edward Goodeve, who was made a baron. On his death their sons, Samuel and John, fell out over the inheritance and became bitter enemies. In 1741 Samuel was in command of a 'man-of-war', the 'Ruby', anchored at Bristol. He discovered that John, who had inherited the title, was by chance also in Bristol. Samuel arranged for John to be enticed on to the ship where he was strangled by two members of the crew. Unfortunately for Samuel, the murder was witnessed. A cooper saw the whole shocking event through an open crevice and his testimony in court led to Samuel and his hired assassins being hanged at Bristol in April 1741. These events seem to have cast a blight on the two remaining members of the family. One died insane and unmarried, the other became a spendthrift and lived to be an eccentric and penniless old man, advertising for a rich wife.

A lane opposite the church gives way to orchards and pleasant hilly country that eventually affords an excellent, if distant, panorama of the 1265 Evesham battle field on the low hills across the Avon valley. The footpath descends to Hampton Ferry and Evesham.

Above: A Saxon cross-head, made of oolitic stone, is displayed inside Cropthorne church. Both faces are richly decorated with foliage, parrot-like birds and a griffin, and a circular recess on one face may originally have contained a jewel. The edge has a rather puzzling Greek-style key pattern.

Although no part of St Michael's Church at Cropthorne is earlier than the 12th century, the Doomsday Book records that the Priory of Worcester provided a priest for the village in 1086, which suggests that an earlier church was in existence at that time. The interior of the church has much of interest, including the painted Dingley tombs, carved choir stalls and a Lady Chapel with an ancient stone slab altar with five consecration crosses.

Right: Ramsons or wild garlic form large colonies in damp woodlands, their presence advertised by the unmistakably pungent smell assaulting the senses.

Right: Blossom time in the Vale of Evesham. Apples and pears have been grown in the region since medieval times, much of the crop being used for making cider and perry.

Above: Holland House, a Retreat, Conference and Laity Centre, in Cropthorne. It was originally three cottages that were combined in the early 19th century. In the mid 20th century a three-storey wing and chapel were added. A sunken garden is reputed to have been designed by Sir Edward Lutyens.

Above right: Manor Cottage and the Old Post Office in Cropthorne.

Right: The Pound House, Cropthorne, The village pound was an area reserved for holding stray livestock until they were reclaimed by the owner.

Ladysmock, a plant with a flower as pretty as its name. It thrives in damp places, sometimes forming large colonies, turning the ground pink.

Mill bridge c1910, Stratford-upon-Avon. Note the goods wagons and signal on the rear bridge. This is now Seven Meadows Road.
Image courtesy of the Shakespeare Birthplace Trust Records Office.

THE RIVER Avon
EVESHAM TO WARWICK

Shakespeare's Forest of Arden

Evesham

A picture on the 13th century seal of Evesham Abbey shows a swineherd in a forest looking up at a vision of the Virgin Mary with the words:

'Eoves her wonede ant was swon
For thi men clepet this Eoveshome'
'Eoves dwelt here and his swine,
Therefore men call this Evesham.'

Eoves was a swineherd of Egwin, the third bishop of Worcester, in the early years of the 8th century. One day, whilst out with his pigs, a sow wandered off into the wilderness. Eoves went in search of her and became lost, before eventually finding the sow only to see her trotting off again, this time into the forest. Coming to an open glade Eoves was granted a vision of the Virgin Mary.

The swineherd hastened back to his bishop to report this experience. The two of them returned to the glade where the vision also appeared to Bishop Egwin. Her words are commemorated on the Abbey seal, 'Ecce locu quen elegi'. 'This is the place I have chosen'.

Bishop Egwin lived in an age of miracles and credulity when reputations could be made on the basis of such events. The overzealous bishop became unpopular in his diocese, perhaps because of his stern sermons against adultery and Sunday working, and was made to account for his behaviour to Ethelred, King of Mercia. The case was referred to the Pope who commanded Egwin to appear before him in Rome.

As an act of penance Egwin fastened a pair of iron horse-fetters to his ankles, locked them and threw the key into the river Avon. This was an astute move, as by the time he arrived in Rome to protest his innocence, his reputation had soared. A fish caught in the river Tiber by one of the bishop's attendants, when cut open, was found to have swallowed the key to the fetters. All charges were promptly dismissed, King Ethelred restored Egwin to his see and gave him the land on which the future vision was to take place. 'Much of the story of the foundation of Evesham', comments the writers of the Victoria County History, 'is doubtless the invention of the 11th and 12th centuries'.

A great Benedictine abbey was built by Bishop Egwin at Evesham but it enjoyed mixed fortunes. When Egwin died in 717, his body was buried in the abbey church and the shrine attracted pilgrims from many parts of Europe. It was destroyed by Danish raiders, rebuilt, but 'fell down' and was then rebuilt and enlarged by a Norman after the Conquest.

There was constant friction during the reign of King John (1199-1216) between the king and the clergy, and perhaps as an act of spite, Roger Norreys, the king's candidate, was appointed Abbot of Evesham, much to the despair of everyone. Norreys, a man previously convicted of misbehaviour at the monastery of Canterbury, took up his new powers with enthusiasm, squandering the abbey's revenues for the next 22 years, until eventually, the Pope, exasperated by such notoriously bad behaviour, deposed him from his position.

Facing page: Abbot Lichfield's tower, built in 1540, shortly before the Dissolution of the Monasteries, is 110 feet high with a through archway. It is lavishly ornamented with battlements, pinnacles and ogee gables. To the left and right of the tower can be seen St Lawrence and All Saints churches, built in the 12th century for Evesham's two parishes so that the Abbey church could be reserved for the monks.

Below: Established by the monks in the 13th century, Hampton Ferry was the means by which they reached their vineyards on Clark's Hill.

Left: This once magnificent archway, now badly weathered, is the Cloister Arch leading to the Chapter House where the monks met every day to hear a chapter read from the Rule of St Benedict. Completed in 1318, the Chapter House was a tall building with ten sides and high windows. It had a stone vault with carved and gilded bosses. Visitors of the time wondered at its beauty and remarked on the fact that the vault required no central column.

Facing page: Abbot Reginald's Gateway, built in the middle of the 12th century, gave access from the market place to the graveyard and the Abbey church. The timber-framed superstructure is late-medieval.

The Almonry where the almoner directed help for local people who were sick or poor. The earliest parts of the building are a 14th century timber-framed hall above a stone basement, and a 14th century stone kitchen. Many alterations have been made over the years resulting in a bewildering patchwork of rooms. The Almonry today is a Tourist Information Centre and heritage museum, with eleven rooms containing displays and artefacts relating to the Abbey, the battle of Evesham, and agricultural and social history.

Hall

Interflora

Right: The Booth Hall, or Round House, built in the late 1400s in the market square, from where there is access to Evesham's new Abbey Gates Shopping Centre.

Facing page: Abbot Lichfield's Bell Tower presides over Evesham's lively High Street. Once a market place for livestock, fruit and vegetables, this exceptionally wide street also housed the town's most prosperous families.

Below: The river Avon at the bottom of Bridge Street, a scene that would have been unrecognisable in the early 1800s, when the river was choked with osier beds and its banks had many busy wharves.

Right: A picturesque house on the corner of Cowl Street and Mill Bank.

The shield of Simon de Montfort, depicted in a stained glass window in Fladbury church.

Left: The Leicester Tower, overlooking the Avon valley and near to the site of the battlefield where Simon de Montfort's army was defeated by Prince Edward in 1265.

On 4th August 1265 the Battle of Evesham raged round the abbey's walls and lands. It was a battle fought between the forces of Henry III's son, Prince Edward, and Simon de Montfort, Earl of Leicester. Henry III's father, King John, had been forced by the barons to sign the Magna Carta limiting the powers of the king under the law. Henry reneged on his promise to abide by the terms of the agreement, and this led to the rebellion of the barons. Simon de Montfort, the elected leader of the barons, captured both Henry and his son, Prince Edward, at the battle of Lewis in 1264. Edward, however, managed to escape and gathered a great army at Worcester.

Guessing correctly that Simon de Montfort would attempt to join his son's army at Kenilworth, the prince decided to march towards Evesham to prevent the baron's progress north. Simon and his army entered Evesham, where they were welcomed by the abbott, but a glance at any map will reveal the folly of the baron's position that night. Evesham is contained within a loop of the river Avon, and the king's army, far superior in numbers, were positioned to cut off Simon's escape to the north. Simon de Montfort was slain in the battle and his mutilated remains were buried in the abbey church. It was popularly believed that he had died a martyr, and for the second time the abbey became famous all over Europe as a centre of pilgrimage. Magna Carta is recognised now as an early step on the road to parliamentary democracy.

The fate of Evesham Abbey at the time of the dissolution of the monasteries was harsher than that of Tewkesbury and Pershore, where at least part of the abbeys were saved from destruction and preserved as churches for the use of the townspeople. Evesham had two parish churches within the walls of the monastery, so most of the abbey was demolished. Abbot Reginald's gateway, built in the 12th century, remains, as does the almonry and the bell tower of Abbot Lichfield. Built shortly before the abbey's destruction, this beautiful tower was erected by the abbey's last abbot.

Rotating sprays watering the crops (and the photographer) at Offenham.

Facing page: The new horticulture at Offenham.

Evesham to Windmill Hill

An hourly local bus service conveniently spared me the necessity of walking there and back through Evesham's suburbs. Evesham's pleasant Bridge Street descends to the bridge over the Avon and becomes the far less pleasant Port Street the other side. Further on, however, a short diversion, signposted 'Ancient Monument' leads to a raised, green, circular island, surrounded by a partially cobbled road, so narrow that it permits one-way traffic only. Old terraced cottages and houses crowd against the road's outer edge, creating the appearance of a small amphitheatre. The grass-covered island is the site of a vanished medieval church. Only a rather grand, but crumbling porch remains, facing Bengeworth Manor across the road, the oldest house in Bengeworth village. A plaque on its wall lists its owners, beginning with King Cnut in 1025, Evesham Abbey in 1207 and the Earl of Warwick n 1268.

The Vale of Evesham is famed for its orchards and market gardens and the greatest concentration of the latter is to be found around Offenham. Footpaths from the edge of Evesham's suburbs thread their way through this, frankly, industrialised horticultural landscape that in places resembles a science-fiction film set. Acres of glass houses are surrounded by even greater areas of plastic sheeting, covering the ground in a landscape denuded of hedges and trees. What it lacks in natural appeal, however, it make up for in interest. The sight of tomatoes and lettuces being grown under glass on an industrial scale

Facing page: The river Avon, turbulent below the weir at the Fish and Anchor. The weir was once a paved ford, and a ferry operated a short way up-river.

Left: Glasshouse cultivation of crops at Offenham.

and being cared for by lonely figures speaking a language that I guessed to be east European, was certainly 'different'. Out in the fields a common sight was that of parked minibuses, their former occupants, Sikhs, in brightly-coloured turbans working their way along rows of vegetables. One group I passed on a morning when a chill wind was blowing from the east, stood in a huddle beside their minibus, looking distinctly unhappy at the prospect of a day spent picking wet broccoli.

In the late afternoon the maze of roads between Badsey, Offenham and the Littletons, becomes for a while choked by monster-articulated trucks, laden with salad crops and vegetables. Some are so long that they have difficulty negotiating the tight corners and junctions, often getting in each other's way as they head for continental Europe.

Offenham's wide Main Street ends at a maypole, one of the tallest in England. A row of seven cottages, built in 1463, nestle under one continuous thatch with the appropriate name of Long Thatch. Twyford Ferry marks the spot on the Avon where the old London road used to cross the river. Relics from the battle of Evesham have been found there, pieces of armour and the bones of men and horses. The most recent find, an axe head, can now be seen in the Almonry Museum in Evesham.

Below: Stitchwort is a fragile-looking plant with pure white flowers that appear to be without support. It is commonly seen in hedgerows associating with red campion and bluebells, the red, blue and white of their flowers the very essence of a British spring.

Below and facing page: A green lane ends where a group of fine stone buildings face each other across a grassy square - church, manor house and tithe barn. Documentary evidence states that the tithe barn was built between 1367 and 1379, but carbon-14 analysis of the roof timbers suggest the earlier date of 1260. The barn's internal dimensions are 136 feet by 32 feet, but these bare facts fail to do justice to this glorious building. A vast, dark, cathedral-like space, thankfully devoid of clutter, bears silent witness to the skills of medieval masons and carpenters who built it,

and the countrymen whose labours filled it every year with the harvest from the medieval fields, as yet unenclosed. It is a sacred space with a congregation of nesting swallows, owls and jackdaws.

This small selection of flowering plants on the Windmill Hill Nature Reserve are an indication of its diversity. As I explored the hill, grasshoppers sprang in all directions, disturbed by my moving feet - a sight that would have been unremarkable in my childhood, but far less common today. The names of wild flowers reveal, perhaps, more effectively than most other means,

Meadow cranesbill

Windmill Hill

Field scabious and Burnet moths

Restharrow

the daily lives of our countryside-dwelling forebears. 'Restharrow', a plant with long swollen roots, capable of halting abruptly a horse-drawn harrow; 'scabious', the herb for treating scabies; 'meadow cranesbill', a plant with seed cases resembling the bird's bill; 'birds-foot-trefoil', known also by many local names, 'eggs and bacon', 'hen and chickens' and 'granny's toenail', the last a mischievous reference to the plant's long talon-shaped seed pods.

Birds-foot-trefoil

Woolly thistle

Windmill Hill to Cleeve Prior

A bridleway on the OS map from Windmill Hill along Cleeve Hill looked inviting, suggesting views of the Avon below. On the ground though, it proved to be a disappointment. Enclosed all the way by trees, the track was evidently regularly churned up by the hooves of horses. Fortunately for me there had been little rain of late so although progress was painfully slow of necessity to avoid a sprained ankle, at least I wasn't sinking at every step into a quagmire. A load of rubble, topped with chippings, and the creation of a few gaps in the west-facing trees would make all the difference. My return journey beside the Avon was far more pleasant, although even there care was necessary in places where the narrow path had crumbled away into the water.

Four teenage boys by the river were throwing a log around in a coltish sort of way as I approached. Turning their attention my way, one leered at me and asked in an offensive manner if I was having a nice day. At that moment a buzzard rose lazily from the branch of a tree on the opposite bank and began slowly circling above. 'Have you noticed that large bird of prey?' I asked, thinking to divert their attention from me to the bird. 'It's a Kestrel', one replied. 'No, its too big for a kestrel, it's a buzzard', I said. 'What would happen to you if you shot it?' another queried. 'You'd have a bad conscience', I answered, more in hope than expectation. Looks of incomprehension all round. I continued on my way . 'Wot's 'e say?' I heard faintly behind me.

Cleeve Prior is the last village beside the Avon in Worcestershire before the river crosses the border into Warwickshire. People have lived here for a very long time, as the discovery of a hoard of Roman coins found by a quarryman in the early 19th century demonstrates. It was one of the largest hoards ever found, 400 gold and 2,000 silver coins, implying the presence of a very wealthy Romanised inhabitant. A historical discovery of a different kind was made in 1824 near the Old Mill. Many skeletons were dug up, thought to be yet more of Simon de Montfort's defeated soldiers from the Battle of Evesham, drowned trying to escape across the river.

In the early years of the 1900s the Old Mill was a popular destination for day trippers from Bidford-on-Avon, often travelling on a fully-laden steam launch towing an equally well-filled passenger boat. One can see why it was such a popular spot when looking at old photographs from those times reproduced in 'The River Avon' by Josephine Jeremiah. One picture features a long line of men dressed in their Sunday best complete with caps, standing on a narrow plank footbridge with a rope handle that crossed the river directly above the weir. Other photographs show the ford in use and visitors to the mill who have arrived by car. When the weir was breached in 1939 it brought about the end of pleasure boating on this formerly deep stretch of the Avon and Cleeve Mill was demolished. Later, even the weir and the ford were utterly destroyed. The site today, sadly, gives not even a hint of its former life. Cleeve Prior derives its name from the gift of the Manor of Cleeve to the Prior of Worcester in 872 by King Alfred's brother, Ethelred. St Andrew's Church is Norman in origin but was heavily Victorianised. Together with the Manor House it lies at the heart of the oldest part of the village.

Left: These deep grooves in the outer wall of St Andrew's Church at Cleeve Prior, are said to be caused by the sharpening of countless arrow heads in former times.

Above: In a field near Cleeve Prior, the latest fashion for horses - a coquettish ensemble of black diaphanous veil and white cape with a black border.

Right: A redundant and decaying gate near Cleeve Prior, engulfed by cow parsley.

Left: The tombstone of Sara Charlett in St Andrew's churchyard records that she died aged 309. The mason spaced the 3 and 9 rather too far apart and helpfully added an O inbetween.

Facing page: The river Avon below Cleeve Hill.

Dovecotes at Cleeve Prior and others beside the river Avon

In the days before refrigeration when most livestock had to be slaughtered and salted before the arrival of winter, doves were a reliable source of fresh meat. The building and owning of dovecotes, however, was restricted to the Lords of the Manor, who might be secular or ecclesiastic, but the crops eaten by the birds were those of their tenants, so this injustice caused considerable resentment. Towards the end of the middle ages, the monopoly of the Church and Lords of the Manor was relaxed, and yeomen also began erecting dovecotes. The earliest dovecotes, probably introduced by the Normans, were round and contained a central pole to which was fixed a ladder, from where the keeper could comfortably reach all of the nests. The arrival of square and rectangular dovecotes appears to have been dictated by fashion as they seem to have been less functionally efficient than the round type. It has been estimated that by the mid 17th century there were, in Britain, approximately 26,000 dovecotes. Saltpetre was extracted from the pigeon droppings and used in the manufacture of gunpowder. Cleeve Prior has two dovecotes. Others exist at Great Comberton, Hillborough Manor, and other parts of the Avon valley.

Below: The dovecote in the grounds of the Manor House, Cleeve Prior, is privately-owned and not open to the public.

Right: A stone-built dovecote beside the King's Arms, Cleeve Prior.

Right: A 17th century dovecote in the beautiful garden of Columbary House, Cropthorne. Visitors are welcome by appointment.

Left: The interior of the Columbary House dovecote showing some of its 1159 nesting boxes. During restoration work two fossilised children's shoes were found, possibly placed there at the time of its construction to bring good luck.

Cleeve Prior to Bidford-on-Avon

The riverside path from the site of the old mill at Cleeve Prior passes through countryside humming with wild life. Although my day there began with grey skies, the clouds evaporated leaving hazy sunshine. Skylarks filled the air with song - a most welcome sound, given their reputedly depleted numbers, and from both banks of the Avon came the incessant churring of whitethroats. Do they ever stop - even in their sleep? One alighted on the stem of a cow parsley beside the river a few feet from me. Blown in all directions by a blustery south-east wind, it clung tenaciously to its fragile perch like some circus trapeze act, never pausing for a moment from its call. Churr... churr... churr ... churr.

The fields hereabouts are composed largely of pebbles, which is not surprising given that they lie at the foot of Marlcliff. In 1969 blasting was resorted to in order to penetrate a solid slab of marl clay and so create a navigation channel for a new lock on the river. It required the combined efforts of a team of Royal Engineers, men from Gloucester Gaol and voluntees, to defeat the obstacle.

A nine-mile riverside footpath from Marlcliff to Stratford-upon-Avon opened in 1987, provided me with a welcome respite from poring over maps, route-finding.

Bidford-on-Avon and Wixford

Icknield Street was constructed in the first century as part of the Roman military conquest of the region. It crossed the river Avon at Bidford where, in recent times, dredging operations have revealed many oak piles capped with metal points that had been driven into the river bed 2,000 years ago by Roman soldiers. Much of Icknield Street lies buried beneath modern tarmac, but a short length of a mile or so, between Wixford and Alcester, exists as a bridleway. Roman roads were a standardised twenty to thirty feet wide, cambered for drainage, with side ditches. This bridleway, although overgrown with bushes and small trees, fits that specification, even retaining at one point a very deep ditch. Along the middle, a narrow track is kept clear by constant use.

The 12th century church at Wixford is situated right beside Icknield Street. Its south chapel contains what Pevsner describes as the finest brasses in the county. Thomas de Crewe and his wife, Juliana, who died in 1411, are depicted on a low altar tomb, he in full plate armour and helmet, she in a dress and mantle with tasselled cords. The church is dedicated to the 7th century St Milburga, one of England's most colourful saints. She was a princess, the grand-daughter of Penda, King of Mercia, and became the first Prioress of Wenlock Abbey in Shropshire. Legend tells that a rejected suitor, inflamed with lust, pursued her with hounds for two days and nights across the Shropshire countryside until she fell exhausted. At that point, her horse kicked the ground and a miraculous spring appeared with which she was able to refresh herself and make her escape. The village of Stoke St Milburga was founded on the spot. Wixford Church is situated on the edge of the once-great forest of Arden. Travellers would collect in groups and assemble at the cross beside the Church to pray for a safe journey. Only the stump of the cross remains.

Facing page: The Crew brasses in Wixford Church. An interesting comparison can be made between this monument and the 17th century alabaster effigies of the Savage family in the church at Elmley Castle (see page 20). Both are outstanding examples of memorial art and craftsmanship, but separated by two centuries, the styles could hardly be more different.

Below: Roman Icknield Street approaching Wixford from Alcester.

Left: Wixford Church and the remains of its cross.

Right: This curious survivor from the early 18th century has hurdle and gorse walls and a thatched roof. It stands in the corner of Wixford Church's graveyard and was used as a shelter for the mounts of visiting clergy. It is a Grade II listed building.

Left: Various river craft moored along the bank of the river near Bidford-on-Avon.

Bidford-on-Avon's bridge, a structure that was already old in 1449 when it underwent repairs, was demolished at the time of the Civil War by King Charles' retreating army. As at Pershore, the destruction of bridges delayed the pursuit of the parliamentary army.

The heart of Bidford is not, as might be expected, near the bridge, but a little way up-river, where can be found the church, the market square and the former Falcon Inn. This is more easily understood when one learns that it was there that the Saxon ford and the Roman crossing was sited. Bidford-on-Avon's earlier name was Byda's Ford and a Saxon settlement is known to have existed there, thanks to the discovery in 1922 of a burial ground. Skilfully-crafted saucer-brooches adorned the remains of bodies that had been buried, as was the custom, with various grave goods. Saxon burials often included iron spearheads, knives, swords, shield bosses (the shield having rotted away), beads, pins and jewellery. The site lies under the Saxonfields development and the public car park.

Modern Bidford-on-Avon feels like a small seaside town. On most days visitors can be seen sitting in or beside their cars parked by the river in Big Meadow, an area set aside for this purpose next to the bridge. Children gravitate to the playground which is safely positioned some distance from the water. Various types of river boats drift slowly by, providing a sedentary form of entertainment. Some stop and tie up, mainly on the opposite bank from where there is easy access to the pubs and shops. On bank holidays and weekends in summer, this relatively small place certainly resembles a seaside town, even down to the smell of fish and chips. It was Shakespeare, apparently, who, with his mates from Stratford-upon-Avon, began the trend of 'a day out' at Bidford. Local tradition claims that the Stratford gang were challenged by a Bidford gang to a drinking contest at the Falcon Inn. The Stratford lads ended up sleeping off the effects under a crab-apple tree on the edge of the village. Next morning some of them wanted to resume the contest, but Shakespeare protested -

'No, I have had enough; I have drunk with
Piping Pebworth, Dancing Marston,
Haunted Hillborough, Hungry Grafton,
Dodging Exhall and Papist Wixford,
Beggarly Broom and Drunken Bidford'.

This bit of folklore was first published in 1762, 146 years after Shakespeare's death, in an anonymous letter to a magazine.

The Market Square, Bidford-on-Avon, with the former Falcon Inn on the right.

Below: Seven-arched Bidford bridge is too narrow to accommodate two-way traffic. Flow is controlled at either end by traffic lights.

Bidford-on-Avon to Stratford-upon-Avon

Apart from a little under a mile of road-walking near Barton, the route follows the riverbank closely all the way from Bidford-on-Avon to Welford-on-Avon. This is a quiet stretch of the river, where my only companions were sheep.

During the coarse fishing season, fishermen line the banks of the Avon. Riverside etiquette requires walkers to pass quietly and not step on their tackle. Most of the common species of fish can be found in the Avon - roach, chubb, dace, tench, carp, perch and pike being plentiful. Bream, up to 10lbs in weight, are caught where the river is slow-moving and deep, whilst barbel find the fast-flowing stretches of the river more to their liking. A more recent introduction, the rather exotic zander, a predator of smaller fish, was introduced from eastern Europe. A member of the perch family, it grows rapidly to maturity in three to four years when the average weight is about 6lbs.

A sprawling modern residential development has appeared, like a rash, round the little village that was once Welford-on-Avon, but the Avon Valley route cleverly succeeds in avoiding this by its choice of paths. Leaving the Avon at the bottom of Boat Lane - a delightful remnant of the old village, full of half-timbered and thatched cottages above a mown grass bank - the route crosses the main road and follows shaded footpaths to Weston-on-Avon.

The 'Four Alls' public house beside Binton Bridges takes its name from 'A King who rules over all; a parson who prays for all; a soldier who fights for all; and a farmer who pays for all'. A narrow packhorse bridge spanned the river and its islands in 1216, but in 1793 the then owner of the islands, William Silvester, demolished the bridge and built a series of small low stone bridges able to bear the weight of wagons. For this service he charged a toll of one shilling. Public subscription in 1804-9 provided the funds to build a twelve-arch bridge, the Welford end of which still survives. The Binton end is relatively modern but a weight restriction of ten tonnes still applies. Two mills existed at one time here, where barges with 30 square foot sails off-loaded coal and took on board osiers (willow twigs for basket-making) and milled grain. The railway line ended all of that before becoming itself redundant.

On a sultry day in June, I stood on the disused railway bridge over the river Stour, watching a shoal of about a dozen quite large fish, envying, for those few moments at least, their cool watery lifestyle. I had followed the Avon Valley route to Stratford-upon-Avon, but hot and tired, had chosen to return along the old railway track, now a cycleway, which was much easier walking than the river bank. Waves of swaying white froth fill the roadsides, lanes and hedgerows of Britain at this time of year. The humble cow parsley is perhaps more responsible for the characteristic look of our countryside than any other plant. Pity about its mousy smell.

A swan with four very young fluffy grey cygnets seemed unconcerned by the oohs and aahs of people strolling along the bank of the river at Stratford, swimming over to see if there was any food on offer. Her cygnets followed closely behind. One cygnet persistently climbed on to his mother's back, so saving himself from the effort of all that frantic paddling. His mother tolerated this for a while, but eventually apparently decided it was in her offspring's best interests to learn to fend for himself, so raising herself vertically with wings outstretched, she tipped him backwards into the water.

The lock and weir at Barton. By the second half of the 17th century the Avon, the first river in England to be made navigable by pound locks, was a busy commercial waterway. The upper Avon from Evesham and Stratford-upon-Avon fell into disrepair during the 19th century, whilst the lower Avon struggled on, suffering from a lack of funds for repairs and maintenance. It was saved by the formation of the Lower Avon Navigation Company Limited, formed in 1924, which carried out immediate repairs but once again, facing funding problems, the company was purchased by C D Barwell in 1949. By the following year the Lower Avon Navigation Trust was formed with him as chairman. During the following decade eight locks between Tewkesbury and Evesham were restored to working order. The Upper Avon Navigation Trust was formed in 1965 with the object of restoring navigation between Evesham and Stratford-upon-Avon. By 1969 over 20,000 cubic yards of spoil from the river had been dredged, and new locks constructed, able to accommodate boats 70 feet long, so for the first time full-length narrow boats were seen on the river. In 1974 the first boats for over a century made the journey between Evesham and Stratford-upon-Avon.

V R
Last Collection Time
Monday to Friday
3.45pm
Saturday
Other Collections

Facing page: A Royal Mail collection box in Boathouse Lane, Welford-on-Avon.

Left: Cottages in Boat Lane, Welford-on-Avon.

Below left: Thatched cottage in Boat Lane.

Below: Thatcher at work on the roof of a cottage at Weston-on-Avon.

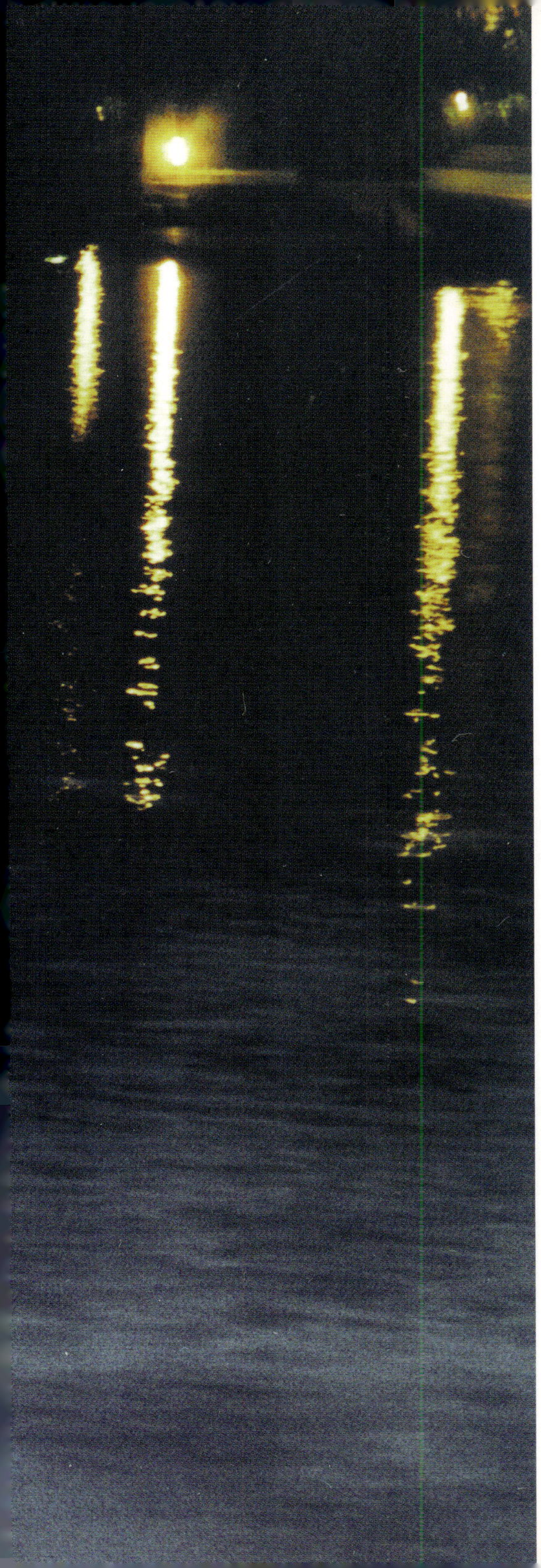

Left: The reflection of the Royal Shakespeare Theatre in the river Avon.

Right: The Gower Memorial in the Bancroft Gardens beside the Avon. The bronze statue of Shakespeare is flanked by four characters from his plays including Falstaff, seen here.

Stratford-upon-Avon

I intend to step carefully round the minefield that is Shakespeare. Fortunately, the poet's world-wide fame is such that there is no need for me to repeat his life and works here. Suffice it to say that without Shakespeare, Stratford-upon-Avon would be just another pretty market town like hundreds of others in the country, and not the focus of pilgrimage it has become, attracting admirers of the poet's works from all round the world. Second only to London as a tourist attraction, Stratford is really quite a small town, often overflowing with visitors to the Royal Shakespeare Theatre and the houses associated with Shakespeare and his relatives.

In 1196, the bishop of Worcester laid out a new town on the edge of an existing Saxon village beside an ancient crossing of the river Avon. It covered 109 acres and was marked out in building plots 12 perches long by 3.5 perches wide, roughly one third of an acre each. Six streets were planned, three parallel to the river and three at right angles to it. This basic plan lies unchanged at the heart of the town today. Although successful - not all planned towns were - by Shakespeare's time Stratford was still a small and leafy town of about 200 houses with many orchards, gardens and trees. A century earlier, one of the town's most successful benefactors, Hugh Clopton, having made his fortune in London, paid for the construction of the bridge near the Avon that bears his name. He also built the Guild Chapel and next to it, for his own use, a house called 'New Place'.

The Guild Chapel, the Guild Hall, the Grammar School, the almshouses and the houses for the schoolmaster and vicar, form the old centre of the town and would have been familiar to Shakespeare. His father was a prominent man in the town, eventually rising to the position of bailiff. He was the town's chief officer, responsible for local order and in charge of the town's properties. But it was his son who was to leave his mark on the town. William went to London where he prospered as a playwright, and by 1613, his life's work complete, he decided to retire to the house he had bought in Stratford a few years previously. This was 'New Place', Hugh Clopton's house, and Shakespeare lived there until his death on 23 April 1616, his 52nd birthday.

Whittard
PONDEN
MILL
MIST
RH04 ERD

Facing page: High Street and Chapel Street, Stratford-upon-Avon.

Right: Shakespeare's birthplace and childhood home.

Stratford-upon-Avon, at the start of the 17th century was, like most other towns, virtually self-sufficient with over forty different crafts and trades and approximately twenty services available. There were 24 tailors, 16 shoemakers, 7 skinners, 5 wheelwrights, 1 fisherman and one collar-maker. Services available included twelve lawyers, six schoolmasters, one physician, one musician and one keeper-of-the-clocks. Over a hundred of the town's inhabitants worked on or owned land, although many of these would also have practised a craft or trade or provided a service.

Boys and girls usually left home at the age of fourteen to become apprenticed with another family for seven years, or became covenanted servants. They were expected to serve their masters and behave themselves in return for learning a trade and being supplied with food, drink, a bed, clothes and shoes. The terms of their covenants were strict: 'Harlottes, dice, cardes or unhonest company or places suspecte or games forbidden he shall not frequent. Matrymony with any woman within the seyd terme he shall not contracte, neither comyt any carnall facte with any mayde servant of his seyd master.'

By the mid 18th century, Stratford's fame as the birthplace and home of Shakespeare had grown to such an extent that tourists crowding round 'New Place' were becoming a source of irritation to its then owner, Rev Francis Gastrell. In 1759, the enraged clergyman demolished the house to spite the tourists, an act for which he paid a high price. He was driven out of the town by the equally enraged townspeople. Stratford's fame as the home of Shakespeare continued to grow, drawing ever larger crowds, to the point where today, the entire town might be considered to be one large shrine to the poet's memory.

Below: The public library in Henley Street.

Right: Mason's Court, Rother Street, one of the oldest surviving domestic buildings in the town.

Right: Harvard House, High Street, was built by Thomas Rogers. Katherine, one of his eleven daughters, married into the Harvard family and her son, John, founded Harvard University in the USA.

Left: In 1596 Shrieves House in Sheep Street comprised a hall, a parlour, a kitchen, buttery and tavern, four bedchambers and two solars.

The Great Garden of New Place, Shakespeare's last home, and the Guild Chapel. Shakespeare's grand-daughter, Elizabeth, and her wealthy husband lived in Nash's House next door.

Old Town Croft.

Above: Shakespeare's daughter, Susanna and her husband, Doctor John Hall, lived in Hall's Croft. It contains a typical 17th century consulting room and John Hall's medical notes, published in 1657.

A ferry crossing the river at Stratford-upon-Avon.

Facing page: Shakespeare is buried beside the river in the Collegiate Church of the Holy Trinity, Stratford-upon-Avon.

Giant hogweed near Ryon Hill House. The hogweed is furtively colonising the river's banks downstream, including a site near Stratford-upon-Avon.

Stratford-upon-Avon to Charlecote Park

Our distant forbears saw little point in creating footpaths that failed to offer practical, social or religious benefits. Paths following rivers are today, therefore, few and far between, unless the river happens to be navigable, in which case, as with the Avon below Stratford, they are rather more plentiful. By contrast, the river Severn which for centuries had trows trading all the way from the sea to Poole Quay near Welshpool, has what amounts to a rudimentary towpath for much of its length. So, reluctantly, I found myself with little choice but to walk along the main road, the A46 to Warwick. There is little good to be said for it, other than noting that it has a serviceable pavement all the way to a minor road to Hampton Lucy, on which I found blessed relief from the constant roar of traffic.

A riverside path is theoretically possible near Oxtalls Farm, but in summer it is almost impenetrable, due to chest-high nettles, thistles, and other vegetation. However, this path does follow the edge of a steep cliff from where there are good views glimpsed between trees, of the Avon below. The path is probably much better in winter and early spring before growth gets going. The views would also be less impeded by foliage on the trees. There is a good reason for this detour in summer. A large colony of giant hogweed has established itself in a sheltered little valley with a brook, near Ryon Hill House. Growing to ten or even fifteen feet high in one season, this spectacular plant can spread aggressively, especially along waterways, and it is an offence under the Wildlife and Countryside Act to plant it in the wild. Furthermore, the plants sap and bristle, if transferred to the skin, cause the skin to become hypersensitive to sunlight, producing painful blisters. Children making blow-pipes with the stems have frequently ended up in the accident and emergency departments of hospitals.

John Leland, writing in the 16th century, described Warwickshire as being divided by the river Avon into two areas. South and east of the river was corn-growing country known as 'the Feldon', whilst to the north and west of the river the countryside was extensively wooded with grassy clearings. This was the Forest of Arden. Shakespeare's maternal and paternal grandparents were yeoman farmers in the Forest of Arden and his experience and knowledge of the area is often evident in his work.

For centuries following the Norman Conquest, the word 'Forest' meant a place of deer, not necessarily of trees also. The concept of Forests was introduced by William the Conqueror, who was proclaiming to his conquered subjects, as well as his fellow Normans, his right to keep deer and hunt them on other people's land. By 1200 there were roughly 150 forests in England, all protected by the law which was enforced by Forest Courts.

Although punishments for infringement were occasionally severe, it was more common for the offender to be fined. In reality, the courts were more interested in raising revenue than exacting revenge. The clearing of woods or encroachment on common land within a Forest was against the law but was often overlooked by the courts in exchange for a small annual payment. One of the ways in which Magna Carta in 1216 curbed the king's abuse of power, was by ending his ever-expanding acquisition of Forests.

There is a disputed tradition that Shakespeare's Justice Shallow in Henry IV Part 2 and The Merry Wives of Windsor is based on Sir Thomas Lucy of Charlecote Park. The text seems to infer that a comparison is being made, especially where the author pokes fun at Shallow's particular foible, his pride in his 'old coat' of arms. It is known that Sir Thomas was prone to boasting of his ancestry. Shakespeare had been caught poaching Lucy's deer and was brought before Sir Thomas, the resident magistrate. The young poet was probably fined and perhaps even flogged. Justice Shallow was perhaps his way of exacting his revenge. The Lucy family are said to have been so annoyed by the caricature that the relevant pages were torn out of their library copy of the plays.

The ancestors of the Lucy family have lived at Charlecote since 1189 or possibly even earlier. Thomas Lucy married a twelve-year old rich heiress, and, using her money, demolished the old family house and rebuilt it using locally-made red bricks ornamented with Warwickshire stone. It is a typical Elizabethan house with octagonal turrets at each corner and on either side of the gatehouse. By the closing years of the 17th century the house had acquired formal water gardens in the Dutch style, laid out by Captain Thomas Lucy, but in 1760 all of this was swept away by Colonel George Lucy, who employed 'Capability Brown' to landscape the park. The river Avon and its tributary, the Dene, became the park's dominant features and the herd of fallow deer, thought to have been introduced in the mid 1400s, were now free to roam within the confines of the park as they pleased.

Personally, I am no great fan of parks, either of the stately homes variety - all grass, lakes and tastefully-positioned trees, or the Corporation Parks Department sort - more grass, ponds and garish rows of bedding plants. I prefer the working countryside of fields, woods and sheep-strewn hills. I hasten to concede, however, that this opinion would probably find little favour with Charlecote Park's many visitors.

Charlecote Park to Warwick

From nearby Hampton Lucy a footpath follows the top of a wooded escarpment rising gradually to Copdock Hill. From the path, there are views to the east over water-meadows grazed by cattle, through which the meandering Avon flows towards Charlecote. It is a landscape pleasing to the eye that compares favourably with any seen along the whole length of the Avon. The view from the top of the escarpment towards the west, however, is very different. Prairie-farmed wheat stretches away as far as one can see. Hedgeless and with only the occasional isolated tree, nothing flourishes there other than corn.

Right: Charlecote Mill dates from the early 1800s. Watermills had appeared in England during the 8th century and by the time of the Doomsday Book there were approximately 6,000. The cost of building and running a mill was considerable, and only the lord of the manor could afford such an investment, the return on which was guaranteed by a monopoly. All of the manor's peasants were compelled to grind their corn at the lord's mill and any handmills or querns found in their possession were smashed by the lord's agents. Peasants paid in kind to the miller, who in turn paid a yearly rent to his lord. Chaucer's miller in The Canterbury Tales, a noisy, ill-mannered cheat who takes three times his share of the corn, reflects the widely held medieval view that all millers were dishonest.

Left: The river Avon between Hampton Lucy and Wasperton.

Facing page: A field of corn on Copdock Hill.

Facing page: The M40 near Barford.

Quiet lanes and a short stretch of the A429 took me to Barford where Joseph Arch was born in 1826. In 1834, when he was eight years old, six farm labourers were tried at Dorchester in Dorset for organising an agricultural trade union. Unions were no longer illegal but the men were charged under the Unlawful Oaths Act of 1797. A hostile judge found them guilty and they were sentenced to be transported to Tasmania for seven years. Vindictive farmer employers, when asked by the men for a raise, had reduced their wages from eight shillings to seven shillings a week - starvation wages, and this had resulted in the men organising themselves.

Both of Joseph Arch's grandfathers were agricultural labourers. Joseph left school aged nine to become a bird-scarer earning fourpence for a twelve-hour day. He was later employed as a ploughboy for three shillings a week, and then as a stable-boy for eight shillings a week. A self-educated man, he became a lay preacher. On 7th February 1872 he walked from Barford to Wellesbourne to address a meeting of agricultural labourers that he estimated to be 2,000 strong, though the local paper put the figure at a more modest 600. The meeting was held in the evening under a chestnut tree by lantern light. He called for a rise of sixpence per day, reduction of the working day to nine hours and the formation of a union.

Joseph Arch went on to speak at other meetings in Warwickshire and in southern England and enjoyed the support of the radical proprietor of the Royal Leamington Chronicle. By March 1872, 200 farm workers were on strike in Wellesbourne, Moreton Morrell, Loxley, Charlecote and Hampton Lucy. Farmers retaliated by organising against strikers and there were lock-outs at Claverdon, Wasperton and Tyso. The workers, however, enjoyed the support of Birmingham which was a centre of radicalism, and Joseph Chamberlain championed their cause in a speech, as well as giving £20 to the strike fund.

Joseph Arch was appointed Secretary of the Warwickshire Agricultural Labourers Union in 1872. In 1885 he became the first agricultural worker to enter Parliament as MP for North-West Norfolk. He retired to the tiny cottage in which he was born at Barford where he died on 12th February 1919.

After Barford there lay ahead of me several miles of road-walking to Warwick and back, followed by more of the same to reach Guys Cliff on the northern edge of the town. The Barford road proved to be particularly unpleasant for walkers, with no pavement on either side, so I had to keep my wits about me, constantly ready to jump into the hedge whenever two large vehicles were passing and we ran out of road space.

Wildlife road-kills in Warwickshire are as common as elsewhere in the country - rabbits, squirrels, hedgehogs, pheasants and the occasional fox and badger. The county also has plenty of deer, and these sometimes end up dead on the roads, as I saw for myself recently when I drove home, passing an exceptionally gory specimen. Completely new to me, however, in this wild-life obituary, was the corpse of an adder lying on its back beside the Barford road in woods below Debden Farm.

Part of the Joseph Arch memorial in the churchyard of St Peters Church, Barford.

One of the sweetest-smelling flowers of the hedgerow, honeysuckle reserves its most powerful scent for night-time when it becomes highly attractive to moths. It is a climbing plant that twines its way up any available support.

Guy's Cliffe in 1935, now an eerie ruin beside the Avon.
Image courtesy of the Shakespeare Birthplace Trust Records Office.

THE RIVER Avon
WARWICK TO RUGBY

Castles, churches and canals

Warwick

The 15th century Beauchamp Chapel in the Collegiate Church of St Mary was built to house the tomb of Richard Beauchamp, Earl of Warwick. His sumptuous tomb, one of the most impressive in England, is unsurpassed for craftsmanship and its use of only the finest materials. The gilded effigy of the earl is cast in latten, an alloy similar to bronze, and is clad in full armour. The knight's head rests on a swan, part of the family crest, and his feet point to a bear and griffin. The bear was a Beauchamp emblem and the griffin an emblem of the de Spencer family. Richard lies on a Purbeck marble tomb surrounded by mourning figures and angels. The mourners are members of the Beauchamp family and include Richard Neville, 'the Kingmaker'. This was a dynasty that from 1268 to the late 1440s were major players in the life of the nation. Their power-base was Warwick Castle.

The earliest fortifications on the site of Warwick Castle were an earthen rampart built in 914 by Ethelflaed, daughter of Alfred the Great. By the 13th century, under Norman rule, the defences had developed into a stone-built 'shell-keep' on an earthen mound, with a rectangular curtain-walled bailey, towers and a gatehouse.

Six generations of de Newburghs followed each other as Earls of Warwick before the line died out. They were succeeded by the illustrious Beauchamp dynasty, Earls of Warwick for the next 148 years.

Thomas Beauchamp (1329-1369) advanced the family's fortunes by becoming one of Edward III's most trusted commanders, fighting at Crecy and Poitiers. He was also military adviser to the Black Prince. At Warwick a massive reconstruction programme was begun by Thomas, which, during the 14th and 15th centuries, transformed the castle into one of the country's most formidable fortresses.

Richard Beauchamp (1401-1439) enjoyed the patronage of both Henry IV and Henry V. He played a prominent role in the defeat of Owen Glyndwr, and in the French wars presided over the trial of Joan of Arc. He was made a Knight of the Garter, the highest medieval honour, by Henry IV, and as the king lay on his deathbed Richard was charged with the responsibility of tutoring the future Henry V. Also a successful diplomat, Richard Beauchamp brought about the union in marriage of Henry V and the daughter of the French king, Charles VI.

This view of Warwick Castle and the Avon, seen from the bridge, has been reproduced many times. It is without doubt the finest vantage point from which to photograph the castle so I was happy to repeat what had been done before. You can't improve on perfection.

Anne, the last of the Beauchamps, married Richard Neville who then became Earl in the time of the Wars of the Roses. He earned from posterity the title of 'the Kingmaker' for his role in deposing both Henry VI and Edward IV.

In 1547, the boy king, Edward VI, the only son of Henry VIII, granted the earldom to John Dudley, whose ill-advised attempt to place his daughter-in-law, Lady Jane Grey, on the throne following the young king's death, backfired tragically. Within two weeks, Mary Tudor had successfully claimed the throne and both Dudley and Lady Jane Grey were executed as traitors. The Dudleys, however, were restored to favour and the earldom by Elizabeth I.

In 1604, following the end of the Dudley line, James I presented the castle to Sir Fulk Greville, whose descendants inherited it down to 1978 when it was sold to the Tussauds Group.

Placed in the centre of the chapel, the earl's fully-armed effigy lies under a hooped hearse intended to support a velvet pall that was only removed on great feast days when mass was said for his soul.

Facing page: The magnificent Beauchamp Chapel in St Marys Church, built between 1443 and 1464 in the Perpendicular style in accordance with the will of Richard Beauchamp, Earl of Warwick who died at Rouen in 1439.

Much might be said both for and against the warrior class of aristocrats who ruled from castles such as Warwick. They lived dangerously, risking everything, including their lives, in the pursuit of their family's interests, which is more than can be said of their effete descendants in later centuries.

In the late 18th century George Greville (the Improver), growing increasingly irritated by the traffic congestion on the narrow medieval bridge over the Avon directly below his castle walls, decided to do something about it. At his own expense, he built a single-span bridge 300 yards up-river and diverted the traffic along a new highway out of the town. His taste for privacy stimulated, he went on to extend the castle grounds, enclosing them with a high sandstone wall. Houses near to the castle were demolished and the old road leading down to the medieval bridge was blocked by this new wall. The pebble surface of Old Castle Street, ending abruptly at the wall, may be seen today. Having satisfied his desire for privacy, George then went on to have the medieval bridge knocked about a bit to turn it into a romantic ruin.

The history of Warwick Castle echoes that of many other stately piles in England. As the real power of the noble families declined, eroded by the rise of the middle classes and parliamentary democracy, they reinvented their ancestral homes as playthings in which to lavish vast sums of money. Armies of servants, gardeners and grooms were required to service these fantasies, often working long hours for little reward. It could not last. Costs were rising and the servants were finding better prospects elsewhere. Finally, with both money and servants gone and the tax man taking his cut, there remained only one option. Downsizing. Many stately homes have now been transformed into visitor attractions, owned by the National Trust, English Heritage or private companies. Their former aristocratic owners sometimes occupy a suite of rooms reserved for their private use or, as at Warwick Castle, have sold up completely and gone. Those with large estates fared better thanks to farm subsidies, combined with a little creative thinking in finding new uses for their houses and parks.

The 14th century chancel and chapter house of St Mary's and the 18th century tower, rebuilt as a result of the fire that destroyed the nave, transepts and tower in 1694. A narrow passageway called Tink-a-tank Lane connects the church to The Butts. The onomatopoeic name comes from the sound made by pattens or wooden clogs worn by townspeople as they walked along the paved alley.

In 1694, fire swept through Warwick destroying much of the town centre. Even St Mary's Church was not spared. The tower, nave and transepts were destroyed, although the chancel, crypt and Beauchamp Chapel were saved. The rebuilding of the town began soon after the disaster and was completed within twenty years. Fortunately, architecture during the reigns of Queen Anne and George I was enjoying a period of refinement and elegance, and although this was in marked contrast to the surrounding medieval timber-framed houses, both styles, at least from our modern viewpoint, sit harmoniously side by side.

Most of the town walls were demolished at this time, but Eastgate and Westgate remain, each with a chapel above. Westgate, a dark tunnel partly cut out of the sandstone, supports the Chapel of St James which dates back to the 12th century. It is adjacent to the much-photographed and filmed Lord Leycester Hospital. This group of medieval timber-framed buildings were acquired by Robert Dudley, Earl of Leycester in 1571 to provide living accommodation for old soldiers.

Beneath the unsuspecting visitors' feet in the yard of The Old Gaol, Northgate Street, there lurks a relic of the darker side of Georgian Warwick life. The period was not all elegance and coffee houses. For over a hundred years, between 1680 and 1797, a hellish dungeon 21 feet wide was in use, capable of holding up to forty prisoners at a time, chained to stone pillars. Their only light came from a circular iron grill in the domed roof, which may still be seen. George Fox in 1662 saw fifty Quakers imprisoned in this evil place for refusing to swear the oath of allegiance to Charles II. The dungeon is not open to the public.

Above: The tower of St Marys, viewed from Castle Street.

Above right: Church Street, with the Athenaeum on the left and the Old Court House, right, built in about 1720. It now houses the town council and the Tourist Information Centre.

Right: Thomas Oaken's House, between Castle Street and Castle Lane, was built in the mid 16th century for a prosperous merchant who was elected Bailiff of Warwick. He left most of his wealth in trust for the relief of the poor of the town.

Facing page: The Lord Leycester Hospital was established in 1571 in a range of 14th century timber-framed buildings by Robert Dudley, Earl of Leicester, as a rest home for soldiers wounded in the service of the queen. From the terrace, stone steps lead up to the 12th century chapel of St James above Westgate.

Top right: The County Museum in the market square was formerly the Old Market House, built in 1670. Its ground floor was open until 1879 when the arches were walled up.

Bottom right: This attractive pool with bird sculptures is situated at the end of the market square.

Bottom far right: A decorative panel of tiles on the Coffee Tavern of 1880 in Old Square, built at the height of the temperance movement.

Facing page: Although the chapel above East Gate was extensively rebuilt 200 years ago, its origins are medieval.

Above: Northgate House, built in 1698.

Below: The Old County Gaol of 1780 remained in use until 1860.

Below: A row of timber-framed houses in West Street.

Below: A cell door from the original gaol in Barrack Street.

Bottom far right: A circular hole with bars was the only source of light into the dungeon, reached down 31 steps from the cell block under the law courts. Circular, with a floor sloping to a cesspit in the centre, it had wooden stakes to which prisoners were chained by leg-irons. It was in use from 1680-1797.

X918 OTW

Above: 'Man traps and Spring Guns on Thefe Premifes', zero-tolerance, old style. A sign attached to a barn at Old Milverton.

Facing page: Mill Street, easily missed by the casual visitor, is one of Warwick's most attractive roads. With a wealth of timber-framed houses and styles of architecture, it is dominated by the Castle's 157feet high Caesar's Tower.

Warwick to Guy's Cliff

I could have used the riverside path from Warwick as far as the Rugby Road, but chose instead to leg it along the noisy Leamington road as far as the bridge over the Grand Union Canal, from where the towpath took me to the canal bridge over the Avon. Here I descended to river level and walked the final few hundred yards to the Rugby road, passing on the way the confluence of the Avon and Leam rivers. One expects to see rather odd-looking, hirsute characters in colourful, slightly shabby clothes on canals but I was left baffled by a party of a dozen or so people that I passed. Men and women, all in dark blue suits, each with an identification tag hanging round his or her neck, they looked like a convention of middle managers from a supermarket on their way to a seminar on shelf-stacking. Where had they come from and where were they going?

Old Milverton sits on a hill overlooking the Avon valley. From the church a well-trodden dusty path, flanked by ripening pods of oilseed rape, led down to the footbridge over the river at Saxon Mill near Guy's Cliff.

The large cave at the foot of Guy's Cliff beside the Avon has been linked with the hero of a once-famous Anglo-Norman 'ancestral romance' from the 12th century. Guy was the son of a Northumbrian nobleman who had fallen on hard times. Seeking his fortune in the south of the country, his character so impressed the Earl of Warwick that he appointed him as his personal steward. Guy soon fell in love with Felice, the earl's daughter, and in order to win her love and be worthy of her, he crossed the English Channel in search of heroic adventures and noble deeds. Returning from Germany, where he had rescued a damsel in distress and won the hand of the Emperor's daughter in a tournament (which he graciously refused, pleading a prior engagement) he suffered rejection from Felice who sent him away to face more adventures. Sir Guy then roamed round Europe, performing many heroic deeds, mostly slaughtering overweight cows, boars and dragons, although he was also credited with relieving Byzantium which at the time was being besieged by Turks.

Returning once more to Warwick, this time Felice accepted him as her husband and when, soon after the wedding, her father died, Sir Guy inherited the earl's estate. If this were a modern romance, the story would end here, but medieval audiences didn't care for happy endings.

Felice became aware that her husband was moping around the place rather a lot and asked what was wrong. Sir Guy replied that he had spent too much of his life trying to win her favour and not enough of it honouring God. So off he went again on his adventures, this time vowing to fight only in just causes and for the love of God. He was away for many years. Felice heard from time to time news of his exploits but eventually, after a long period without news she assumed that he was dead. She grew old.

It was her custom each day to give alms to beggars at the castle gate and one day a stranger showed her a ring that she had given Sir Guy before his departure. Astonished, she questioned the man closely and begged him to take her to its owner. The stranger led her across fields and down to the river to the entrance of a large cave, inside which Sir Guy lay close to death. With his last breath he told Felice that he wanted to see her one more time and had sent the ring so that she might come and close his dying eyes. So he died in Felice's arms. Unable to face life without him (although we might suppose that she had grown accustomed to it by now), Felice climbed to the top of the cliff and leaped to her death in the river.

Left: The river Avon beneath Guy's Cliff, scene of Felice's suicide in the medieval romance.

Facing page: The eerie ruins at Guy's Cliff are the remains of a mansion built in the middle of the 18th century. A 14th century chapel on the cliff contains a large medieval stone sculpture of Sir Guy.

Clarendon Square. Refined mid-19th century elegance in the heart of Leamington Spa.

Royal Leamington Spa

Leamington's saline springs were known to the Elizabethan Antiquary, Camden, in 1586, but remained unexploited for the following 200 years, until Benjamin Satchwell arrived in 1787. By the early years of the 19th century several baths had been established and were attracting patrons. In 1801 Leamington had only 315 inhabitants, but by 1841 the population had risen dramatically to almost 13,000. It had become a fashionable place to live, thanks to its reputation as England's premier spa town. Planned as a grid with the Parade its main street, intersected at right angles by Regent Street and Warwick Street, the area was sub-divided into side streets, terraces, crescents and squares. Standing in one of these squares and admiring the simple effectiveness of its plan I questioned why this and others like it had not been taken up by architects and town planners in subsequent years right down to our own times, as an example to follow. Four-storey terraced houses facing each other across a green square that serves as a recreation area seems such a successful solution to high-density living. The space enclosed creates its own refuge from traffic and noise for both people and wildlife. It would be difficult, I grant, to match the superb architecture of these squares, and such elegance comes at a price, but I see no reason why it could not be scaled down whilst retaining the principle. The problem, of course, rests with us, the house buyers. We prefer a semi with a bit of garden front and back.

The popularity of the baths at Leamington grew in the early years of the 19th century to the point where demand was outstripping supply, and in 1814 the Pump Room Baths were officially opened at a cost of nearly £30,000. The season for drinking the waters stretched from May to the end of October. By 1830 it cost three shillings and sixpence to drink waters for one week, ten shillings for a month and 21 shillings for the season. More favourable rates existed for families. A cold bath might be had for one shilling and sixpence but a warm bath cost three shillings.

Dr Henry Jephson, a popular physician, set up a practice in the town in 1828 attracting many blue-blooded patients, including the young Princess Victoria, later Queen Victoria. Dukes, duchesses, princesses and other titled persons soon followed and in 1838, the Queen authorised the town's use of 'Royal Leamington Spa' as its official name. For 50 years Dr Jephson's benign influence was a great asset to Leamington which has remembered him with the Jephson Gardens, laid out in 1875. Today, the gardens are a popular destination on a sunny day for mothers with young children, the elderly seeking a change from daytime TV, and office workers snatching a lunch-time break.

Right: Leamington Spa's Town Hall, built in the latter part of the 19th century, is a mixture of Tudor and Baroque styles.

Facing page: Royal Pump Room and Baths, viewed from the Jephson Gardens.

Right: This terrace, another example of the town's assured architectural elegance, is within sight of the Royal Pump Room and Baths.

Facing page: The Jephson Gardens Glasshouse, opened in 2003, has collections of plants from the Old World - Africa and Asia, and the New World - the Americas, Mexico and Australia.

Right: A house by the river Avon near Hill Wootton.

Guy's Cliff to Stoneleigh

Blacklow Hill is an innocuous-looking leafy mound near Guy's Cliff and Saxon Mill. Hidden among its trees is a memorial to Piers Gaveston who was beheaded there on 1 July 1312 by barons resentful of his influence over Edward II.

The woods and fields beside the Avon below Hill Wootton, and the delightful little village of Ashow further up river are oases of calm within a labyrinth of interconnecting main roads filled with frenetic motorists. Even so, rarely did I escape the stereophonic sounds of traffic and the vibration of hot rubber on melting tarmac.

Stoneleigh Abbey began as a small community of Cistercian monks in 1154 on land given to them by Henry II. Following the Dissolution, the abbey eventually came into the possession of Sir Thomas Leigh who, in 1558, became Lord Mayor of London, and in the following year was knighted by Elizabeth I. He began to build on the abbey site, but died in 1571, leaving the work to be completed by his widow, Dame Alice, and his son, Thomas. Their building was incorporated into the east wing of the 18th century Italian-style house that we see today. A handsome gatehouse, erected in 1346 by the sixteenth Abbot, Robert de Hockele, with Elizabethan modifications, stands near the house.

Jane Austen's mother was first cousin to Rev Thomas Leigh, who in 1806, on learning that he had inherited the Stoneleigh estate, invited his cousins, including Jane, to join him on a visit to inspect the property. A description of it appears in her novel, 'Mansfield Park' in chapters eight to ten, where the house is called 'Sotherton Court'. It also appears in 'Northanger Abbey', and in letters to her family, Jane described the view south over the river Avon and parkland.

Facing page: Woods beside the river Avon near Hill Wootton.

Right: Naturally high in nitrogen, these fields of borage were destined to be ploughed into the ground, so releasing fertiliser for the following crop of wheat. The farmer receives a grant for planting borage from the EEC. Borage is used in some herbal remedies and oil from its seeds is used for the treatment of cardiovascular reactivity to stress. The flowers are candied for culinary decorations and frozen in ice cubes for cocktails.

Right: Ashow's Church of the Assumption of Our Lady.

Facing page: Ashow is one of the hidden little gems of Warwickshire. A narrow road flanked by red brick and timber-framed cottages ends at the village church where a path, with a wall one side and a hedge the other, leads to a mown churchyard that slopes down to the banks of the Avon. Crossing the churchyard and taking a few steps beyond the shade of a tree that marks the point at which the path is resumed, one arrives at a footbridge over the Avon with views across wide flat green pastures.

The village of Stoneleigh was a welcome sight, signalling the end of that part of the route begun at Barford that necessitated miles of unavoidable road walking along busy highways. From Stoneleigh the remainder of my chosen route to the source of the Avon would be along footpaths, country lanes and canal towpaths.

Stoneleigh is a village characterised by timber-framed cottages infilled with red brick, although other types of construction can also be seen. It has several cruck-framed cottages - far more than most villages - and it also has many box-framed cottages. Built originally with open hearths and a hall open to the roof, by the 16th century the peasant owners were able to afford to install brick chimneys which, in turn, made possible the insertion of upper floors and stairs. Brick cladding replaced wattle and daub. All of Stoneleigh's cottages were converted and improved in this way, often with the addition of extensions in the form of extra bays and wings.

St Mary's church beside the river Sowe, in the shelter of Motslow Hill, is 12th century Norman, built with red sandstone quarried from the nearby hill. It has a richly decorated Romanesque chancel arch with zigzags and horizontal clasps, and on each supporting column is a tiny (I am tempted to say 'cute') bird and an equally tiny snake. Outside, the north doorway is also splendid, although badly weathered. Featured on its tympanum are two barbaric interlocked dragons biting their own tails, and above, two much smaller snakes doing the same. The late 11th or 12th century font is reputed to have come from Maxstoke Priory where it lay for over 250 years in a dung heap.

The Leighs of Stoneleigh Abbey left their mark on the village down the years, notably with the almshouses of 1594, built by Alice, wife of Sir Thomas Leigh. Like the church, they are constructed with sandstone from Motslow Hill. In 1850 more almshouses were built on the opposite side of the green by Lady Leigh. Other benefactions from the Leighs include a school, estate cottages, and a coach house that later became a reading room with a library of 750 books and, more recently, the village club. The blacksmith's smithy on the green, no longer in use, was built in 1851, but it occupies the site of smithies going back to John Capp who from 1599 to 1640 provided the village's needs, making and repairing tools, pots and pans, ploughshares and weapons, as well as shoeing horses.

Right: A blocked doorway at St Mary's Church, Stoneleigh, has a tympanum with dragons and snakes.

Left: Stoneleigh's 16th century Manor Farmhouse was originally L-shaped, but acquired a wing during the 17th century.

Right: St Mary's font is encircled by the twelve apostles within a tight-fitting arcading.

Above: Almshouses bearing the date 1594, built by Alice, wife of Sir Thomas Leigh, in the centre of Stoneleigh.

Examples of a cruck-frame cottage, left, and a box-frame cottage, right, at Stoneleigh.

Above left: Kenilworth Abbey's Gatehouse, the only substantial ruin from the former Abbey that was confiscated by the king in 1538.

Above top: The barn, the last remaining building from the Abbey, was used for the storage of grain. It may also have been a brewhouse or a fish house.

Above: The entrance to St Nicholas' Church, Kenilworth, is believed to have come from the Abbey, perhaps at the time of the dissolution.

Kenilworth Castle

'Chinewrde' in the 1068 Doomsday Book, but Kenildewurda' by 1165, the oldest part of the town of Kenilworth is the cross-roads, a little to the north of Finham Brook which is a tributary of the river Avon. Its High Street leads directly to the castle some little way to the west. The parish church of St Nicholas has a richly ornamented late 12th century west doorway that probably came from the nearby abbey. Kenilworth Abbey was a priory for Augustinian Canons established by Geoffrey de Clinton in 1122. It was a wealthy house, valued at over £500 at the time of the Dissolution in 1540, when its church and all but one of its domestic buildings were demolished.

In July, 1575, Elizabeth I was entertained for nineteen days at Kenilworth Castle by her favourite, Robert Dudley, Earl of Leicester. For her amusement a pageant-master unrolled a programme of fireworks on the vast artificial lake surrounding the castle. There was bear baiting by dogs, Italian acrobats, hunting expeditions and a play about a massacre of the Danes in 1002. This lavish spectacle was staged in and around a castle that had been at the heart of English history since its construction 460 years earlier by Geoffrey de Clinton, chamberlain to Henry I.

By the end of the 12th century Kenilworth Castle had a large keep and a protective curtain wall with towers. At that time it was royal policy to reduce the number of castles owned by barons, and Kenilworth was one that fell into the king's hands. This policy

Facing page: Kenilworth's High Street.

FOR SALE
BOOTHROYD
(01926) 857244

Facing page: The Great Hall of Kenilworth Castle, viewed from a track leading to the site of Henry V's Pleasaunce House.

Right: Ruins of the Inner Court, Kenilworth Castle.

infuriated the barons, who resented the growing concentration of power under the crown and it was one of the factors that led to the revolt culminating in the signing by King John of Magna Carta.

However, John managed to hang on to Kenilworth and between 1210 and 1215 he paid for additional fortifications. These were principally the building of an outer perimeter wall with towers at intervals and the creation of a shallow lake. The conflict between the king and the barons continued during the reign of Henry III. Simon de Montfort, leader of the barons' revolt, had custody of the castle at this time, but following his defeat and death at the battle of Evesham his son, also called Simon, fled to Kenilworth and prepared for the arrival of the king with his army and the inevitable siege, which proved to be the longest in English history. The castle's defences had been cunningly devised, so that the siege continued for almost nine months, but the castle's occupants were eventually forced to surrender owing to an epidemic of disease and for want of food.

By the middle of the 14th century, Kenilworth Castle was in the hands of John of Gaunt, the future Henry IV. He spent a lot of time there and was responsible between 1389 and 1394 for the building of a palace that overlooked the lake. His son, Henry V, found the new buildings too noisy for his taste and constructed a Pleasaunce house well away from the castle in a marsh.

By 1553 John Dudley owned the castle, and although he forfeited both his head and his castle for treason against Catholic Mary Tudor, the castle was soon restored to his handsome son, Robert, by Mary's successor, Protestant Elizabeth I. This was the high point of the castle's fortunes. Robert added further buildings within the perimeter walls, including stables and an outer gatehouse. He also created a pleasure garden.

Following the Battle of Edgehill during the Civil War, Kenilworth Castle fell into Parliamentary hands and was 'slighted'. The outermost wall of the Keep was blown up, and the wall of the Out Ward was breached. So began the castle's gradual decline to its present state as one of England's noblest and most romantic ruins.

Top left: Kenilworth Castle from the site of the former artificial lake.

Above: Castle Green, Kenilworth.

Right: Under the flight path of a plane flying out of Coventry Airport.

Stoneleigh to Ryton-on-Dunsmore

Motlow Hill was a welcome, though brief, return to hill country, the first since Bredon Hill many miles back in another county. Dotted about this area are some very old oak trees with mighty girths. Many appear to be thriving, showing no sign of decay, and may well once have been part of the Forest of Arden. The river Avon, yet to be united with water from the rivers Sowe and Leam, is unrecognisable as the same river at Warwick or Stratford. In fact, as I made my way up-river, in some places it was little more than a brook. Reassured by 'Centenary Way' signposts, my guides as far as Bretford, I entered a recently-cut hayfield full of rolypoly bundles of hay scattered around ready for collection. From nearby Coventry airport came the sound of aero-engines revving, preparing for take-off, followed by a roar and the sight of a plane lumbering into the sky. I walked on, pushing through uncut hay at the edge of the field and sending up clouds of small butterflies.

Facing page: Stare Bridge is late medieval, with nine arches, only three of which span the river Avon.

A Green Man in Bubbenhall Church.

Facing page: The river Avon at Cloud Bridge.

The parish church of St Giles at Bubbenhall has two late 13th century foliate head corbels, or as they are usually called, 'Green Men'. The Green Man was probably the most common decorative motif of medieval sculpture, found on capitals, fonts, corbels, tympana, misericords and bench ends throughout the country. Exeter Cathedral alone has seventeen Green Men. Foliate heads or leaf masks first appeared in the Roman empire during the 2nd century AD, finding their way into churches slowly at first but, from the 5th century, part of an established tradition. Their interpretation is open to dispute. Some claim they represent nature's power of regeneration in springtime, whilst others say they are demons or lost souls, warnings to the congregation of God's judgement to come.

The 'Nature's Regeneration' theory perhaps fits those examples where a face peeps out at us from behind a tangle of foliage, such as the one that can be seen in Pershore Abbey, but most Green Men, it must be admitted, are, to say the least, disquieting and some are positively horrific. Perhaps both explanations are valid, some periods stressing the rebirth of nature, others the fear of hell and damnation. One thing is certain, the masons and other craftsmen embraced the motif with enthusiasm. It gave free reign to their imaginations and enabled them to display the full extent of their skills.

'Sir Gawayne and the Grene Knight' is a 14th century working of the Green Man theme in literature. The story was ancient at the time of the poem's composition, probably originating in remote Celtic times. A huge figure, dressed all in green and on a green mount, intrudes into King Arthur's Christmas revels at Camelot on New Year's Day. Sir Gawayne accepts the stranger's challenge to combat and strikes off his head with an axe. The Green Knight leaps up, picks up his head and mounts his horse, inviting Sir Gawayne to a return combat in a year's time at the Green Chapel. Sir Gawayne receives hospitality at the Green

Knight's castle, but while the castle's owner goes hunting, Sir Gawayne is tempted on three successive nights by the Green Knight's young wife. He resists her approaches but secretly accepts a green girdle from the lady, for which betrayal of the Green Knight's hospitality he suffers a slight injury in the combat that follows. Returning to Arthur's Camelot, Sir Gawayne recounts his adventures to the amused court who from then on wear green girdles in commemoration of his exploits.

From Bubbenhall there followed a rather dull landscape of vast wheatfields and little else, which nevertheless had the merit of peace and solitude. This gave way abruptly to Ryton-on-Dunsmore, trapped in its triangle of major highways, complete with urban underpasses. A 'first' for me was following the 'Centenary Way' across a colossal holding area for thousands of unsold new cars freshly manufactured at the sprawling factory nearby. However, Ryton-on-Dunsmore ended as abruptly as it had begun and a few yards into a field of barley I was startled by the sudden explosion at my feet of a dozen or so partridge into the air, uttering shrill alarm calls, their wings whirring and their bright chestnut rumps very distinctive.

The Avon near Ryton-on-Dunsmore reminded me poignantly of a river I lived near to as a boy, the Corve, in Shropshire. Like the Corve, it had steep tree-lined banks a few feet high between which the river hurried over stony or sandy beds and around clumps of rushes, forming little islands. Elsewhere, dark pools provided refuge for fish that quickly darted away into their mysterious depths, while shoals of small fry congregated in shallow water so clear they might have been suspended in air.

Returning through Bubbenhall and approaching the church, I was passed by a man emerging from the churchyard pushing a platform trolley. He was dressed in an all-enveloping silvery-white shell suit of the kind worn by forensic scientists at scenes of crimes. The hood was up and his face was hidden by a black fine-meshed net. On his trolley was a large box-shaped object wrapped in material identical to that worn by the man, but poking out of the top was a shape that may or may not have been a beehive. The man, the trolley and its load got into a car and were driven away by a third party. I was nearing the end of that day's journey and was feeling tired but surely not so tired as to be hallucinating.

Above: Sunlight glinting from the headlamps of countless rows of new unsold cars, parked on a vast holding area at Ryton-on-Dunsmore.

Facing page top: The wild rose, England's national flower, blooms in June and July, the culmination of the season's floral procession. Other flowers might follow, but none more beautiful or with such a history.

Right: The heart of old Wolston, with its pretty rill and bridges. The village is now encircled by modern housing estates.

Ryton-on-Dunsmore to Bretford

A large shoal of small fish, the biggest about six inches long, swam in a shallow area of the Avon at Wolston. From a footbridge beside the road bridge, I watched the arrival of two girls in their early teens, pushing their cycles over the grass to the river's edge. They produced a bundle of bread and began tearing it into little pieces and throwing it to the fish. No wonder the shoal was large. As I studied the deeper water below me, a fish much bigger than any I expected to see in a river this size, glided majestically into view among the lily pads. Plump and about fourteen inches long, it must have weighed several pounds.

Wolston, for much of the last two centuries, consisted of a single main street lined with 18th century houses. A straight rill down one side of the street has little bridges at intervals providing access to and from the houses. In recent times the village has grown to many times this size and now consists mainly of modern housing estates. The 11th century St Margaret's church beside the Avon is within hailing distance of extensive earthworks on the opposite bank that are all that remain of Brandon Castle, built in the 12th century. For many years it was a seat of the de Verdon family, before being destroyed by the barons during their conflict with Henry III, after which it was repaired and used again until about 1309.

Bretford to Little Lawford

Bretford, where the Roman Fosse Way crosses the river Avon, was founded in 1227 by the de Verdons, lords of Brandon Castle, but it failed to prosper. Bretford bridge is mentioned in 1279 and is known to have been repaired in 1653, following damage during the Civil War. At Bretford two towers become visible on the eastern skyline, one is the Rugby Cement Works, the other a ruined church tower at Kings Newnham. It was the latter to which a narrow lane with passing places was leading me. Kings Newnham, or Newnham Regis, is a village that became depopulated in the 16th century when John Dudley, the Duke of Northumberland, enclosed the common lands. The ruined tower is all that is left of the village's church, St Laurence, the nave and chancel having been pulled down in 1794. The bells were taken to St Mary's at Monks Kirby and the font became an ornament in the garden of the Hall.

Three ponds next to Newnham Hall were constructed by monks from Kenilworth Priory to provide the brothers with fresh fish. Terraced out of the hillside, today's anglers sit beside the pools, shaded from the heat of the mid-day sun by large green umbrellas. A strange tale is told of Kings Newnham. Following heavy rain one day in the mid 19th century, it was noticed that water in the rickyard, formerly the churchyard, drained away unaccountably quickly. Digging near the old church tower revealed a water-filled family burial vault containing the coffins of the Earl of Chichester, Lady Chichester, Lord Dunsmore and Sir John Anderson. Of greater interest, however, was an un-named coffin containing the remains of a man who had been beheaded. The head had been placed beside the body and round the neck there was a black silk ribbon embroidered with the initials TB. All of the bodies had been embalmed and covered with rosemary and other herbs. The coffins were re-sealed and returned to the vault.

A field path from Kings Newnham goes directly to the nearby village of Church Lawford, crossing the river Avon over a modern footbridge. Here I found the remains of a watermill. The building had gone, but there were a few rotting timbers, rusting wheels and cogs which together with extensive earthworks made a mental reconstruction of the site relatively easy. The river ran clear in and out of reed beds and was alive with fish of differing sizes, although none more than about nine inches long. Above the water, turquoise-blue damsel flies flew, criss-crossing the river, sometimes coming to rest with folded wings on a reed blade. Their much larger relatives, the dragonflies, were a wonder to watch. Flying at speeds between 35 and 60 mph they would stop suddenly, as though hitting an invisible barrier, hover, and fly off at an acute angle to their former flight path.

Another macabre story is attached to the next village up-river, Little Lawford. In 1780, the owner of Little Lawford Hall, Sir Theodosius Boughton, was slowly poisoned by his brother-in-law, Captain Donellan, who hoped to inherit the estate, but instead ended his life on the gallows at Warwick. The Hall was demolished in 1790.

Above: Getting in the harvest, near Bretford.

Facing page: The ruined tower of Kings Newnham Church.

Below: Poppies love disturbed ground, the seeds sometimes lying dormant for many years then suddenly appearing as if from nowhere. The plant has always been closely associated with cornfields, and until herbicides almost wiped them out it was a common sight to see whole fields of wheat splashed with the vermilion flowers. They have now been banished to the fields' edges.

Poppy seeds have been found among 4,500 year old relics from Egypt, and for many ancient cultures the plant's powers of regeneration were associated with fertility. Statues of the Roman Ceres, goddess of agriculture, were decorated with poppies and wheat or barley. As agriculture spread round the world the poppy came with it.

Facing page: A fisherman enjoying the warmth of a setting summer sun beside pools created by monks from Kenilworth Priory.

Left and far left: Remains of a watermill at Kings Newnham.

Below: A footbridge over the Avon at Kings Newnham.

Right: Little Lawford's ford over the Avon.

Right: Orange Balsam, a native of North America, enjoys the distinction of being first discovered growing wild in Britain by the philosopher John Stuart Mill in 1822. Its seeds float readily on water, colonising the banks of the Oxford Canal where it is quite common.

Above: Rugby Cement Works, unmissable for miles around.

Right: St Botolph's Church, Newbold-on-Avon.

Right: James Brindley's Oxford Canal, opened in 1790. It is now a popular waterway for a variety of river craft.

Above: A boat about to enter the Newbold Tunnel at Newbold-on-Avon

Little Lawford to the Oxford Canal

From Newbold-on-Avon I chose to use the towpath of the Oxford Canal to take me on my way towards Clifton-on-Dunsmore. The Oxford Canal was the last to be built by that indefatigable canal engineer, James Brindley, who died during its construction. Work began in 1769 at the canal's northern end near Coventry, and following its completion at Oxford, it was opened in 1790. The first true canal had been constructed 200 years earlier between 1564 and 1567 at Exeter, but no further canals were attempted until 1760, when the Duke of Bridgewater commissioned Brindley to build a canal to carry coal from his mines at Worsley to Manchester. Brindley became obsessed with canal-building, often working on several at one time. Josiah Wedgewood, the potter, who took an interest in Brindley's work, wrote in 1767, 'I am afraid he will do too much & leve us before his vast designs are executed; he is so incessantly harassed on every side, that he hath no rest, either for his mind, or Body, & will not be prevailed upon to have proper care for his health ...'. In 1772, at Ipstones in Staffordshire, Brindley lay in a damp bed in damp clothes, was taken ill and discovered to have diabetes, which together with a kidney infection, proved fatal.

The Oxford Canal, like all early canals, followed the contours of the land. Later canals were made as straight as possible by means of cuttings, embankments and tunnels. Sometimes older canals were straightened by later engineers, as happened with the Oxford Canal, which was shortened by 13.5 miles and included the Newbold Tunnel, built in the 1820s, as part of the straightening process. By the 1830s over 4,000 miles of canals and other waterways criss-crossed England, but during the following decade, serious competition arrived in the form of the railways. By 1850, 6,000 miles of track were in use, causing a decline in the use of the canal network. Rugby enjoyed the distinction of being an early railway town with tracks converging there from the north-west and the south-east.

Elderberries and elderflowers are the ingredients of two of our best-loved country wines, one red and one a fragrant white. A refreshing cordial is also made with elderflowers.

Mary Gilbert of the George Inn on her narrowboat in 1907, with her daughters Gwen and Julia. The 'Gwen Mary' ferried coal, coke and other goods up the arm of the Grand Union Canal to the wharf at Welford, to be delivered by cart to surrounding villages.
Image courtesy of Barry Crowther.

THE RIVER Avon
RUGBY TO NASEBY

Reed-filled rills and ridge and furrow

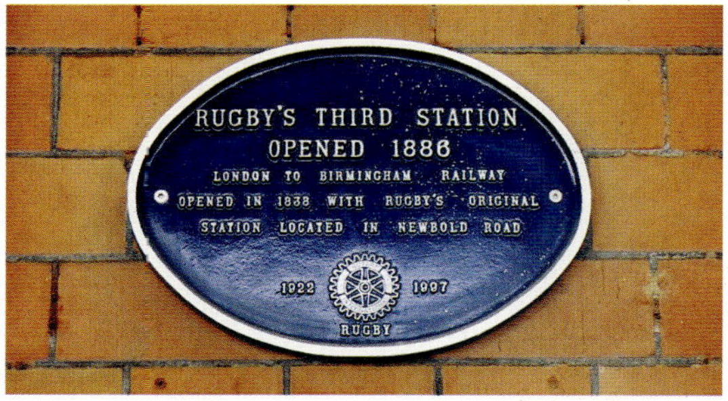

Rugby

At the time of the Doomsday Book, Rugby was a mere hamlet in the parish of Clifton-upon-Dunsmore. Its Saxon name 'Hroca's burg' had been modified to 'Rocheberie' by the Danes and it wasn't until the 18th century that the present name of 'Rugby' was finally established. In 1255 it had been granted a weekly market by Henry III, but even by the early 19th century, Rugby was little more than a large village. Two developments dramatically altered this situation: the growing reputation of its public school and the construction of the London and Birmingham Railway in 1838. The line, engineered by Robert Stephenson, started at London and went via Rugby and Coventry to end at Curzon Street Station in Birmingham, where connections could be made to travel on to Liverpool and Manchester on the Grand Junction Railway. This became known as the 'West Coast Main Line'. In 1846 it was part of the London and North Western Railway and from 1840 the company provided through connections from London to Leamington Spa, Leicester and Peterborough. These lines were axed during the 1960's Beeching cuts.

The first station at Rugby was a temporary wooden building which lasted only a few years until the creation of a junction in 1840, when a new station was built near the site of the present one. This was owned by two railway companies, London and North Western Railway and Midland Railway and consequently was poorly planned, resulting in platforms that were too low for the convenience of passengers. It was a busy, noisy, chaotic place, depicted under the fictitious name of 'Mugby Junction' by Charles Dickens.

The town's second station was closed in the 1880s following the construction of a new line to Northampton from Rugby and was replaced by the present station in 1885 which has one of the longest platforms in the country.

Facing page: An intercity train arriving from the west at Rugby station.

Rugby School was established in 1567 under a bequest of Lawrence Sherriff, a staunch supporter of Princess Elizabeth during the troubled reign of her sister Mary, for which loyalty he was rewarded when the Princess became Queen. The school was intended to be a free grammar school for the benefit of the children of Rugby and Brownsover, and was endowed with estates in London and Rugby. The first building was situated near to the Market Place, but between 1740-1750 the school moved to its present site where it quickly developed under the leadership of Dr Thomas James, headmaster from 1768-1782. The school's reputation became firmly established under the headmastership of Dr Thomas Arnold between 1828-1842, whose methods influenced the whole system of public school education.

In his 'Buildings of England - Warwickshire', Pevsner remarks acidly that 'No-one would call the first sight of Rugby School from the town cheering'. He goes on, however, to heap unqualified praise on the architect William Butterfield who was commissioned in 1867 to design New Quad and the Chapel. Much of this programme of new building was achieved thanks to the leadership of the then headmaster, Dr Frederick Temple, later to become Archbishop Temple. New buildings continued to appear during the latter years of the 19th century and the early years of the 20th.

Rugby School is, of course, famous for the invention of the game of Rugby. In 1823 a sixteen-year old pupil, William Webb Ellis, 'With a fine disregard for the rules ... first took the ball in his arms and ran with it'. For centuries prior to this, a savage kicking game had been played in which players kicked each other as much, if not more than the ball, often ending up with serious injuries. Change, however, arrived slowly and it was not until 1845 that an official attempt was made to formulate rules.

The school has educated many famous luminaries, including Matthew Arnold (son of Dr Arnold), C L Dodgson (ie Lewis Carroll), Archbishop William Temple, Rupert Brook and Wyndham Lewis.

'There's more to Rugby than Rugby ...' declares one of the town's information leaflets, but to the casual visitor, Rugby may appear somewhat overawed by its public school, an infant prodigy that grew into a sprawling pedagogic giant. Rugby's 'Pathway of Fame' waymarked route was created for the Rugby World Cup in 1999 and is an excellent way of exploring the town, with interpretation signs along the way and a booklet to accompany the walk, full of information. But, as one would expect of such a project, it tends to reinforce the impression that the town comes a poor second to the public school and the game of Rugby. Perhaps the town's most celebrated son, other than masters and scholars who went on to make names for themselves, is Sir Frank Whittle. He invented the jet engine, the first of which was built at the British Thompson-Houston factory and Brownsover Hall in 1937.

Facing page: Rugby School and the William Webb Ellis statue sculpted by Graham Ibbeson and unveiled by Jeremy Guscott in 1997.

DUNCHURCH ROAD

Above: Rugby School Close, birthplace of the game of Rugby Foootball.

Right: William Gilbert made his world-famous Rugby football on these premises in 1842. It is now a museum of Rugby memorabilia.

Left: This statue of Thomas Hughes, author of the semi-autobiographical Tom Brown's Schooldays, stands in front of the Temple Reading Room, the Rugby School Library.

Facing page: High Street and Rugby School. Now pedestrian-ised, High Street has developed a pavement cafe culture.

SCAFFOLDING
0121-772 1712
07979 245 213

Above and above right: Two of Rugby's old inns. Originally two cottages, the Squirrel was built in the 18th century.

Right: Rugby's modern Art Gallery, Museum and Library contains Roman artefacts found at nearby Tripontium and a collection of modern art.

Oxford Canal to Lillebourne

Leaving the Oxford Canal at the point where it passes over the river Avon, I found myself crossing a field of very pronounced medieval ridge and furrow. I was heading towards a large arch in the embankment of a demolished railway, the first of two former railways in the short distance between the canal and Clifton-upon-Dunsmore. The OS map of the area shows five abandoned tracks as well as those still in use. The Avon, only a few yards wide here, varies constantly between being a recognisable small river and little more than a reed-choked ditch.

From Clifton upon-Dunsmore a farm lane followed by field paths took me to Lilbourne, passing at first through a field that contained half-a-dozen bullocks. Frisky and intent on jostling me from behind, which I at first ignored, their attention grew increasingly daring, so with a shout and a bit of arm-waving I watched as the group stampeded to the far corner of the field, kicking up clouds of dust like a scene from a low-budget cowboy movie.

Roman Watling Street is the point at which my route passed from the county of Warwickshire into Northamptonshire, with the course of the river Avon forming a further county boundary between Northamptonshire and Leicestershire to the north. Watling Street ran from the south-east coast of England, via London, to Viroconium (modern Wroxeter) and for a time on to Chester and North Wales. A Romano-British town, Tripontium, approximately one mile to the north of my route, was originally a military frontier post established around AD50. It had an administrative building, a hotel and a large public baths. There is no public access to the site but finds from the archaeological excavations are on display in the Rugby Art Gallery and Museum. Watling Street remained a significant landmark after the departure of the Roman legions, becoming the boundary drawn up by treaty dividing Saxons in the south-west of the country from Danes in the north-east, the Danelaw. Centuries later Thomas Telford revived Watling Street, turning it into a 19th century turnpike road. Today, Watling Street, or the A5, is busier than ever, as I can confirm having stood on its edge waiting to cross and being buffeted by the repeated rush of displaced air from convoys of heavy trucks.

Becoming slightly lost and seeking my way through a field of wheat stubble growing between sharp-edged lumps of flint, I was startled by a hare springing to its feet almost as I was about to step on it. Running down towards the Avon and swerving from side to side, it was easily distinguished from a rabbit by its larger size and black-on-white tipped long ears. Overhead, two buzzards circled above the small wood to which I was heading. At its highest point, about 300 feet, the hill has a motte and bailey overlooking a steep descent to Lilbourne church. In between, the hillside is covered with ridge and furrow, whilst behind the church I could see the substantial remains of another motte and bailey, this one far more extensive than its neighbour at the top of the hill. Why, I wondered, were two so close to each other? Perhaps the one by the church replaced the one on the hill? A brief notice in the church porch drew my attention to a blocked Saxon arch in the chancel wall and suggested that the earliest Christians would have been baptised in the nearby river Avon. If it was as choked with reeds then as it is now, I mused, they would have been hard-pressed to find a patch of clear water.

As a backdrop to this scene of Roman and medieval history, the M1 slices through the landscape, rushing towards its interchange with the M6 a mile to the north for all points west and the A14 arriving from the east.

Below: Tunnel in the embankment of a dismantled railway near Clifton-upon-Dunsmore.

Facing page: The river Avon near Clifton-upon-Dunsmore.

Left: Plants swaying in the current of the river.

Below: St Mary's Church, Clifton-upon-Dunsmore.

Services
WIDNEY CABS Ltd
NORTHAMPTON

Facing page: Roman Watling Street, now the modern A5, near Lilbourne.

Left: Traffic on the M1 and a Norman motte and bailey at Lilbourne.

Left: A drinking hole in the Avon is shared by cattle in adjacent fields. In the distance, Lilbourne's motte and bailey.

Facing page: A blocked Saxon doorway in All Saints Church, Lilbourne.

Right: A rare clear stretch of the Avon flowing towards its underpass of the A14, near Stanford-on-Avon.

Lilbourne to the Grand Union Canal

Craneflies in biblical plague numbers flew around me as they were flushed out of the long grass by my feet trudging up and down the ridge and furrow fields between Lilbourne and Stanford-on-Avon. A map pinned to a gatepost showing local footpaths was prefaced with the information that this was the most extensive area of medieval open-field ridge and furrow in the region, information that my weary legs fully endorsed though didn't necessarily welcome. Although still full of reeds and other plants, the river Avon in these fields has been cleared in places by farmers to create access to water for cattle and sheep. Little fenced-off areas of running water attract shoals of fish, all about four to five inches long and often numbering twenty or more.

Stanford Hall, an outstanding example of William and Mary 17th century architectural style, was built for Sir Roger Cave, whose descendants have lived there ever since. It replaced an earlier manor house. Stanford Hall is in Leicestershire but the parish church of St Nicholas, containing many memorial tombs of the Cave family, is over the border (and the river Avon) in Northamptonshire. This impressive church, built in the early 14th century, replaced a Norman church which itself had replaced a Saxon church. William Laud, vicar of Stanford in 1607, rose to be Archbishop of Canterbury.

Left: The early 14th century Church of St Nicholas, Stanford-on-Avon.

Facing page: The focal point inside most parish churches is the east window above the altar. Stanford-on-Avon's church has two focal points, the second being this splendid organ at the west end. Belonging originally to Charles I, it stood in the Chapel Royal at Whitehall Palace. Following the king's execution, the organ was sold by Cromwell to Magdalen College, Oxford, where it proved to be too small for their needs. Bought by Sir Thomas Cave in 1649, it was brought here and installed above an oak gallery supported by two classical pillars. The Church also contains a collection of armorial hatchments to the Cave family, claimed to be the finest in the county.

Two deserted village sites are marked on the OS map of the area, one at Stanford and the other, Downtown village, beneath Downtown Hill. I decided to see if anything remained of the latter and followed the canal towpath which passed the site. If I had hoped to find, as at other such sites, evidence on the ground in the form of house platforms and a holloway, I was to be disappointed. A large ploughed field, gently sloping away from the hill, appeared to be completely devoid of features. The village and its occupants alike have been eradicated from history.

Returning along the towpath, my attention was caught by a tiny dot on the water, followed by a narrow wake, moving at right angles from the far bank to my side of the canal. Curious as to what such a small creature might be, I walked quietly on to the point of its destination. Ripples in the water showed that it was moving slowly along the edge of the canal. Then I saw what it was. A grass snake, about eighteen inches long with its head held just above the water. Its body, barely beneath the surface, was looping from side to side propelling it forwards. From its mouth a tiny forked tongue flicked intermittently, presumably testing the air for the scent of prey. I have seen several grass snakes over the years and I know they are perfectly well adapted to life in water, but this was the first I had ever seen swimming.

Left: The Grand Union Canal near Hemplow Hills.

The Grand Union Canal to Welford

From the Grand Union Canal I followed the Jurassic Way up Hemplow Hills and on to Welford where I fell into conversation with a villager. He advanced the novel theory that 'his' Welford had a greater claim to call itself Welford-on-Avon than the village of that name in Warwickshire, on the grounds that the Avon nearer its source was unadulterated by tributary rivers and streams. Looking over the road bridge later that day at the marshy expanse of reeds I knew to be the Avon, and comparing it mentally to the wide river at Binton Bridges near Welford-on-Avon, with its islands and flowering water lilies, I couldn't help reflecting that my friend's loyalty to his village, although commendable, as a campaign was unlikely to be successful.

Welford originally had three parallel streets, the main road being the modern West Street. The most westerly of the three, together with the medieval houses, has long gone, leaving only mounds and hollows and a fish pond. The parish church of St Mary the Virgin dates from the 13th century, although an earlier church is thought to have existed. Evidence for this appeared when a 12th century priest's chalice was dug up in the churchyard.

During the 17th and 18th centuries the village enjoyed a period of relative prosperity, thanks to its position on the coach road midway between Leicester and Northampton. Some of the High Street's houses are former coaching inns. Like many large villages, Welford was self-sufficient, with blacksmiths, wheelwrights, butchers, bakers, drapers, tailors, shoe-makers and other tradesmen.

The Welford arm of the Grand Union Canal terminated at Welford Wharf, beside the Avon and the turnpike road. It was a centre of industrial activity with a mill, a lift bridge, the George Inn (now the Wharf Inn), limestone-burning kilns and a busy coal yard. Water from the Naseby, Sulby and Welford reservoirs, constructed between 1815 and 1837, was fed to the Grand Union Canal along the Welford arm.

Facing page: Stanford Reservoir is fed by the waters of the river Avon, which then continues on its way through the parkland of Stanford Hall.

Left: The Doctor's House, Welford, so called from the days when it was occupied by a succession of doctors. A stone in its handsome exterior records that it was built in 1687 by John Woodford.

Right: The river Avon flows under several small farm bridges in fields between Welford and Sulby Abbey.

Above: Barges moored at Welford Wharf.

Right: High Street, Welford.

Left: Sloes are the fruit of the blackthorn tree, commonly used as hedging, its vicious thorns making an impenetrable barrier. Although looking like a very small plum, anyone who has ever tasted a sloe will know the difference; sloes are extremely bitter. They do, however, when pricked with a pin and dropped into a jug of gin with a little sugar, make excellent sloe gin.

Below: The site of 12th century Sulby Abbey, destroyed in 1538.

Welford to the River Avon's source at Naseby

A flash of metallic azure blue and it was gone. The kingfisher had been perching on an iron post, waiting for a passing fish when I looked over the low stone wall of the bridge. It had been within touching distance as I crossed the Avon on the road to Naseby.

Two parallel branches of the river flow down the valley from Naseby, one natural and one man-made, carrying water to replenish the canal. Very different from the sluggish meandering reed-filled ditch on the planes, these channels of clear water flow rapidly through meadows populated by sheep and cows, cutting narrow passages through thick carpets of water plants growing between low banks of red earth. To call them alpine streams would be an exaggeration, but that is the comparison that springs to mind.

A footpath follows the Avon to the site of Sulby Abbey, founded in 1155. Extensive earthworks indicate that, at the time of its destruction in 1538, it was a place of considerable importance. But like many other religious houses it fell victim to the ferment of controversy during the Reformation and Henry VIII's need of revenue. A letter to Thomas Cromwell , the king's minister responsible for the dissolution of the monasteries, describes Sulby as 'the papistical den of idle and utterly unlearned beasts'.

On rising ground to the east of Sulby Abbey, above Sulby and Welford reservoirs, is the site of Old Sulby, a village that was probably decimated by the Black Death in 1348, although it managed to struggle on for a further hundred years. Unlike Downtown, where nothing remains, earthworks covering a wide area remind us of the generations who lived out their simple lives here and called the place 'home'.

The Civil War battlefield of Naseby lies about a mile to the north of the village from which it takes its name.

'If you choose godly honest men to be captains of Horse', said Cromwell, 'honest men will follow. I had rather have a plain russet-coated captain that knows what he fights for, and loves what he knows, than that which you call a gentleman, and is nothing else'. Cromwell's 'Ironsides' had been well-drilled and taught to charge without breaking formation when pursuing an enemy. They also had the unshakeable conviction that God was on their side. At the battle of Naseby in 1645 Parliamentarians enjoyed the advantage of outnumbering the enemy by two to one.

King Charles' troops, attired in shining breastplates and velvet livery, were successful at first, forcing the Parliamentary foot soldiers to give way, but confusion ensued in the heat of the battle when Charles, attempting to rally his troops, gave the impression to his cavalry that he was about to withdraw, and withdrawal turned into a rout. The King lost all of his guns and his baggage train containing booty with an estimated value of £100,000 in gold, silver and precious stones. He had, in fact, also lost his kingdom and was ultimately to lose his head.

Charles I had alienated many of his subjects by his autocratic attempts to rule his kingdom without the aid of parliament. Also, his religious persuasions were regarded by puritans as being those of a papist. He was married to a Catholic and his Archbishop of Canterbury, William Laud, was sympathetic to the old faith. The Archbishop's attempt to force a new prayer book on the Scots was the cause of the first military action, forcing Charles to recall parliament in order to raise taxes for war in Scotland. Parliament ended in farce when Charles, attempting to arrest five radical members, found the door shut in his face. The country became divided between those who supported the king and those who supported parliament. Often, brothers, fathers and cousins found themselves facing each other on the battlefields and there was much bloodshed. Proportionally, in fact, there was a greater loss of life during the Civil War than in the Great War of 1914-1918.

Following his defeats at Naseby and Langport, Charles refused to accept Cromwell's compromise proposals and was, indeed, secretly plotting a renewal of hostilities. This led to the second Civil war in 1648 when the King's army once again was defeated. A thoroughly exasperated parliament, believing that there could be no peace while Charles lived, determined to get rid of him. He was tried and executed in January 1649.

Attempts by Charles II to regain his father's throne in 1650-1651, were quickly overcome, but Cromwell's reign as Lord Protector proved to be less than popular with either those loyal to the crown or puritan zealots, and a mere eleven years after Charles I's execution, Charles II was invited by parliament to reclaim the throne. The absolute power of kings had gone for good and parliament's powers had been enhanced, but what a tragic loss of so many lives for such a messy compromise.

A pillar in a small enclosure marks the site of the Civil War Battle of Naseby in 1645.

Above: Trees on the skyline at Naseby.

Right: A track between Naseby Reservoir and Naseby. A ditch at the edge of the field on the right is the infant Avon.

Above: All Saints, Naseby, contains 'Cromwell's Table'. A group of Royalist soldiers are reputed to have been eating at the table in Shuckburgh House, opposite the church, when they were surprised and captured by a party of Parliamentary scouts.

The setting sun on a late autumn day over the Avon valley near Naseby.

Below: This is the river Avon's first appearance above ground, in the garden of a private house.

The giddy height of 600 feet above sea level held the prospect, I hoped, of finding the infant Avon to be clear and fast-flowing, racing over pebbles and sandy beds, and down little waterfalls. But mountain stream it most definitely was not. Between the dam of Naseby reservoir, where a stagnant-looking outflow enters a dark concrete tunnel under the A14, and the river's source at Naseby, the Avon is but a drainage ditch running along hedged boundaries of fields.

Although not the official source of the river, the Avon's first appearance from beneath Naseby is in a private garden, where a trickle of water drops from a pipe into a verdant gully flanked by green ferns. A decade or more ago the river made an earlier appearance, bubbling up through the stone floor of the cellar of an old inn opposite the parish church, but building alterations blocked the flow.

Naseby is an ancient village, its earliest name Hnaefesburgh or 'the fortress of Hnaef' suggesting an early Saxon settlement. Best known for its connection with the Civil War, signs direct those interested to a small museum on the edge of the village, where relics from the battlefield are displayed.

Many springs in the district might claim to be the source of the river Avon, but Naseby enjoys the distinction of the official title. A cast-iron cone in the grounds of the manor house opposite the parish church marks the spot, and I can think of no more appropriate beginning than a garden, for a river that flows through meadows, orchards and market gardens.

The official source of the river Avon is marked by this cast-iron cone bearing the inscription, 'Source of the Avon 1822'. Springs have a habit of moving and this one seems to have dried up. A villager commented that he had lived in Naseby for ten years and never seen a drop of water in it. Situated in the grounds of the manor house opposite the parish church, it may easily be viewed by looking over a low roadside wall.

The new bridge over the river Avon at Pershore.

From his home in Worcestershire, John Bradford has extensively explored, on foot and invariably with a camera, the counties of Herefordshire, Shropshire, Gloucestershire and Powys, as well, of course, as his own county. The river Avon flows through parts of England that John is very familiar with, nowhere more so than Bredon Hill, to which he frequently returns. The Avon in Warwickshire and further east was new and stimulating territory for him which resulted in some of this book's most attractive photographs. As both graphic designer and photographer, John aims to produce memorable pictures of the English and Welsh countryside, attractively presented in well-designed books. His photographs have appeared in two previous books, *Worcestershire, a portrait of the county* by Sam Redgrave, published by Halfshire Books, and *The River Severn, a journey following the river from the estuary to its source* by John Bradford, first edition published by Hunt End Books, second edition by Brewin Books.